PREPPER COLLECTION

4 BOOKS IN ONE TO HELP YOU PREPARE FOR DISASTER

DAVID NASH

PREFACE

Since you are reading a book on self-reliance, I am assuming you want to know more about how to take care of yourself in disaster situations

I would like to suggest you take a moment and visit my website and YouTube channel for thousands of hours of free content related to basic preparedness concepts

Dave's Homestead Website
https://www.tngun.com

Dave's Homestead YouTube Channel
https://www.youtube.com/tngun

Shepherd Publishing
https://www.shepherdpublish.com

21 DAYS TO BASIC PREPAREDNESS

SIMPLE THINGS YOU CAN DO TO PREPARE FOR ANY EMERGENCY.

DAVID NASH

INTRODUCTION

There are quite a few schools of thought when it comes to personal disaster preparedness. The largest seems to be concerned with "Stuff". I call this the government model. In this model, practitioners buy gear to solve problems. They seem to feel that money equals solutions.

While you do need to have some level of resources, I feel this is a mistake, because stuff can get stolen, damaged, or lost. If you rely solely on gear, then no matter how redundant you think you are, you still have a single point of failure.

I believe in a balanced approach. In this document, I will illustrate basic concepts for disaster preparedness as well as give you some solid tips and steps to help you begin to prepare.

There is very little in the way of gear acquisition written in the following pages. You will need to acquire some measure of food, water, and equipment if you are to become more disaster resilient, however, there are multitudes of resources on and off line to help you do just that.

What is this book is designed to do is to guide you through the first steps of personal preparedness, i.e., "getting your mind right". I find that without a solid set of guideposts, it is easy to fall down the rabbit hole and concentrate only on buying stuff, or gaining training. Both of which are necessary, but neither will allow you the flexibility to adapt, improvise, or overcome.

Venn diagram of the relationship between skills, stuff, and training

I want you to be balanced, to have the right mix of things *and* skills with a strong mindset to be able to thrive in any situation.

I do not have all the answers, but I have spent decade's figuring out the best solutions for my family. Everything I wrote in this eBook are things I have done, and it has worked well for me. Take it as a guide and a starting point, question everything, and find your own solutions.

I have taken the liberty of writing this as if we were sitting in your living room talking; it is informal because preparedness does not have to be stressful.

Please do not mistake my familiar terms for ignorance of the subject. I have a degree in Emergency Management, hold certification as Emergency Management Professional, and have over a decade in planning and teaching Emergency Management in state service as well as a lifetime of doing this with my family.

1

ESTABLISH THE PROPER MINDSET

❖

I t is no secret that I believe a proper mindset is vital to thriving in times of difficulty. In movies, Hollywood depicts typical prepper scenarios where there is no doubt that the characters are in disaster situations. In the real world however, it probably won't be so clear-cut. The popular survival concept of WROL (Without Rule of Law) is, in my opinion, a fantasy. The government has plans and procedures in provide continuity of government. What this means to you is that there may not be a clear cut signal that,"the balloon is up" and its time to change into camouflage and start carrying your AR-15s and AK-47s.

This makes mindset extremely valuable. Prepping should be integrated into your lifestyle. Preparing to surmount obstacles allows you to have a longer and better life, it is not supposed to take over your life. If being involved in prepping doesn't make your life easier, then you are doing it wrong.

Prepping is insurance for things I am either not able to fix, or cannot afford to fix on my own.

I live in the New Madrid Seismic Zone. Without a doubt, that is the largest natural threat I have. In the event we have a large-scale quake, and the infrastructure is disrupted long term, I may not be able to go to the store to buy food. That bothered me, so I took steps to learn how to grow my own food. Each new skill I learned, and each packet of seed I put back lessened my worry. I still have the Earthquake as my largest natural threat, but I am not scared of it, because I have done all I can do to be prepared for it.

Another key to the mindset of prepping is to look at your resources from an "all hazards approach". I was a prepper long before Y2K, and will be one long after 2012. I don't prep for single emergencies. I know that the seeds and food I have stored in the event of a catastrophic earthquake would also work if I lost my job, or got hurt working on some crazy project. Try to build capability and skills, rather than just work on specific threats.

Be flexible, during the Great Irish Potato Famine, only the potatoes were affected by blight, field corn, barley and oats were not. However, people starved to death while having barns full of alternative foods because they could not bring themselves to eat "horse food". I have made it a habit to look for alternative uses for products, not because it is efficient or cost effective to use things outside of their designed uses, but because it incubates mental flexibility. Historically, the ones that thrive in hard times are the quickest to adapt. - Which means - BE FLEXIBLE.

Lastly, cultivate a mindset that incorporates a tiered approach to skill and gear acquisition. All to often, I see people that have top of the line (and expensive) equipment in one area, but nothing in other essential areas. A $6000 dollar sniper rifle and 10,000 rounds won't do you any good if you freeze to death because your electric furnace doesn't work. Make sure to be balanced. Get some food, the ability to make shelter, purify water, and defend yourself. Then get more food, and better equipment. Keep this up, and soon you will have that fancy rifle, but you will be able to stay comfortable and well fed also...

The very first step is to take a moment and think about why you are interested in prepping and what you would do to protect what you love.

2

HOLD A KICK OFF MEETING

Prepping is a lifestyle, and nothing changes lifestyle more than marriage. If you are married, or have people in your household that depend on you, then you must communicate with them.

If you do not, then you will regret it. I find that the more my wife understands about what I am doing and WHY I do it, the more she supports the direction I am leading the family in.

It is very important that after you have thought about why you want to prepare, you sit down with your loved ones and share that with them. "Honey, I love you and the kids more than anything else in life, and I worry that if something bad happened I would not be able to keep you safe. Would you help me take some steps to ensure that no matter what happens, the kids will never be cold and hungry" will make your life infinitely easier than, "Look, you just don't under-stand, and I don't have time to explain it, when the postman comes, just sign for the package, and put it in my office."

Get everyone's input. In the emergency management world

this is called stakeholder support. If your loved ones feel like their concerns were listened to, and that they have a stake in the process, then they will most likely be more willing to sacrifice in the short term for long range results.

It is also important to get their input to ensure that you are not missing anything, that you have all the information, and that your plan is realistic.

If you ignored the mindset page, and are prepping solely for and anticipation of a commie zombie invasion that was launched after a huge solar are wiped out the national electric grid, your spouse probably won't go along with that. You should probably listen to them and compromise a little.

Go back about mindset, and look at "all hazards". A small kit to get you through a winter ice storm can serve you use in a zombie apocalypse, and it keeps the door open for upgrades over time. Failing to heed your spouse's concerns, ignoring them, and refusing to compromise ensures that each time you spend family resources on becoming more disaster resilient you are seen being in the wrong.

Involving everyone, working together, and communicating ensures that your actions are perceived in the manner they are intended, that you are a loving provider that is taking responsibility for those you love.

The more eyes on the problem, the more solutions you will receive, and the more willing your family will be to actually practice the plan you came up with together.

Step two is to block out some time when everyone that lives in your home can sit down and discuss the idea of becoming more disaster resilient. I suggest that you share your reasoning for feeling the need to prepare, and let them share their feelings. If everyone is not on board, then do not pressure them or get offended. Being a positive role model will do much more to get them on board than badgering them will. I will say, I have experience with both models, (and one divorce...). At this point you are only opening the dialog.

Remember, prepping is not a sprint, it is a marathon. Please don't overdo it, or make it overly formal or you will probably only get frustrated and quit.

3

MAKE A THREAT ASSESSMENT

Making a threat assessment is a vital part of making a comprehensive disaster preparedness plan. If you don't know what can make you have a bad day, then you have no idea how to keep from having a bad day. Now I know that a few pages ago I made a big deal about taking an All Hazards approach to prepping, and now it may seem that I am changing midstream, but I am not.

We want out preparations to work for as many types of hazards we can, and we don't want to obsess on a single threat to the exclusions of all others.

The more we know about what can happen, the better we can focus our efforts. During this threat assessment we want to take a deeper look at anything we are worried about, as well as anything that came out of the kickoff meeting. Historical information from the local emergency management agency, and past Presidential disaster declarations (available from FEMA), also helps.

I have been trying to find a way to go to the FEMA Tsunami course they give in Hawaii, but since Tennessee is not threatened by Tsunami's I cannot justify spending any resources to prepare for that type of disaster.

Performing a threat assessment is about looking at likely threats and comparing them by how much they would impact you. This allows you to prioritize them so that you can better allocate your resources.

	Impact	Likelihood	Threat
Asteroid	10	1	5
Cuts and Scrapes	1	10	5
Home Invasion	9	3	6
New Madrid Earthquake	8	6	7
Tornado	7	5	6

A large asteroid impacting the planet would kill everyone - Impact 10, but it is unlikely, so it gets a 1 for likelihood.

I cut and burn myself regularly as I build projects, but it is rarely very serious, so impact 1, likelihood 9

This is a pretty unscientific chart, but it does a good job of showing the relationship of Impact and likelihood.

By averaging out likelihood with impacts, I can see that preparing for an earthquake or tornado is a better use of my resources than trying to figure out how to survive an asteroid impact. If I wanted to go really in depth, and make a much more useful, albeit complicated chart, I could factor in the cost to prepare, and the effectiveness of such preparations. If I did that, then asteroid impact would clearly be the least of my worries, but Home Invasion, and Tornados would both rank higher on the matrix.

Today, spend some time working on the threats that could impact your family. If you live near a highway, consider hazardous material spills, or flooding, if you live in low-lying areas.

Once you have your assessment done, you can move toward either decreasing those threats as well as preparing for them if they do occur.

4

MITIGATE ALL THREATS POSSIBLE

Once you have identified the threats that could impact your family, then the smart thing is to reduce the impact as much as possible. In emergency management mitigation is the effort to reduce loss of life and property by lessening the impact of disasters. Would you rather spend money on reducing the impact of a disaster, or fixing the damage after the fact.

I will give you an example, since earthquakes are higher on my list, I ensure that the rigid connectors (like at my water heater) are replaced with flexible connectors so that the lines won't break if shaken, and that my bookshelves are connected to the wall using nylon straps screwed to the shelf, and to a wall stud.

For home invasion, or other criminal threat, I have a plan in place, a nice alarm system, and other details that tell a criminal he would be better o trying another house.

This step will require some homework. You have to know

what is likely to happen, as well as what you can do to prevent it.

I would suggest that you look into the Federal Emergency Management Agencies free independent study program. They have a course called **"IS-394.a Protecting Your Home or Small Business From Disaster"** that will explain how protective measures can reduce or eliminate long-term risks to your home and personal property from hazards.

Other resources for mitigation strategies would be your local and state emergency management agencies. I know that sometimes government grants are available for certain mitigation strategies.

After the Alabama Tornadoes of 2011, my in-laws used grant funding to have a safe room constructed at their home.

A good earthquake mitigation is installing water heater strapping

While it is a larger scope of mitigation, one of the reasons the Haiti earthquakes were so catastrophic was that local building codes were not-enforced, and the local concrete was mostly sand. The same issue of cost came into play for hurricane sandy. Flood protection is costly, so it is almost nonexistent in New York. However, the cost of the flooding dwarfs the cost of mitigation.

Mitigation is insurance, pay a little now, and hope you never have to see a benefit, or save a little now, and possibly pay a lot later.

PRIORITIZE YOUR ACTIONS

Hopefully your mitigation steps have lessened the impacts of disasters to the point that the list of things to do is much smaller. Once I mitigated the threat of criminal trespassers by buying an alarm, a dog, and a shotgun, I don't have to spend a lot of time worrying about it. Now I can spend my limited prepping resources on other threat types.

The next step is to take the modified risk list and look at what gives me the most bang for the buck. I can spend around $30-50 and have a pre-made 72 hour kit shipped to my door in under 15 minutes of internet shopping, or I can spend half that and go to the store and build a kit specifically designed for me. Depending on if time or money is more valuable to me.

It is very easy to achieve a minimum level of preparedness. A 72-hour kit, and some basic knowledge is the minimum recommended by FEMA and the Red Cross. A deeper level of preparedness takes more work, and it is important to know that no matter how much you spend you will never be fully prepared for every disaster.

What you need to do now is to sit back down with your spouse and look at the chart and decide if you want to go after the easiest things first, or the areas that have the most impact.

1945 Wartime Poster

Personally, I went for the easy first, both because of my all hazards ideal, and because the small wins kept the momentum going to keep my wife on board with prepping.

Something that is very important to remember when doing your prioritizing is that you are prepping because you love and cherish your family. If you spend all your time prepping, you may be neglecting them at the same time.

I have a list of things we need to buy, do, or learn to reach that next tier of preparedness, but I also know the things my wife feels are important for our family. While I am very conscious of the dollars spent, and hate to see any money wasted when it could go to preps, I also know that spending a reasonable amount of money on family entertainment isn't going to cause us to all die during the zombie apocalypse.

Personal preparedness is a balancing act. To little, and you are irresponsible, too much and your a twice divorced kook. Hitting a balance can be difficult, but it is worth it.

ASSESS AVAILABLE RESOURCES

The next thing to do, after you prioritize the actions you need to do to take to prepare for disasters, is to look at your resources. Typically when people hear the word *resources* they thing in terms of money or "stuff". That is part of it, but time, energy, and knowledge are also resources.

You can find ways to prepare cheaply, quickly, or effectively. You can even manage to do two of these things, but except in very rare circumstances, you are not going to be able to have all three at the same time.

One of my favorite authors is a man named **David Gingery**, his books are about making your own metal working tools, in an interview I read, Mr. Gingery spoke of how as a poor young machinist, he was often presented with problems that typically were solved with $500 solutions. Gingery said since he never had $500 he had to use his mind creatively to solve the same problem with $50. I am not a machinist, and if I tried to be I would turn a $500 problem into a $50000 problem by wreaking the machine. What I do have is the willingness to make mistakes, and a large library of books from people who have solved similar problems. That means I can leverage other people's knowledge, and experiment and tweak to t my situation.

If I had a lot of money fall into my lap, I would use that resource to quickly buy the things I need to hit the level of preparedness I would be comfortable with, but since that is unlikely, I have to go slowly and prepare incrementally.

My wife and I have an understanding, and I know exactly how much I can spend without impacting the grocery budget. She trusts my judgment, and knows that I have an overall plan. So I am free to make the purchases we need without a lot of oversight, but to make it simple I have a list of the things we need for the current preparedness tiers and the next few tiers above that. This list contains what things cost, what is a good deal, and what price is too good to pass up.

That way, If I happen on a yard sale or somebody offers me something they don't want I can very quickly determine if its worth spending the resources on.

A full pantry is comforting, but you also need skills

Preparedness is not about buying things; true preparedness is about building capabilities. Too much stuff can be almost as bad as not enough. Most of the people killed in natural disasters like hurricanes, ignored evacuation orders so that they could stay home and protect against looters.

What you need to do is to determine how much time, money, and energy you are willing to dedicate to becoming more disaster resilient. Some weeks you will spend more, and sometimes less, but pick a number that you are comfortable with and stick to it.

7

MAKE A PLAN

You may have been wondering why this took so long to get to the planning process, but in all actuality you have been making your plan all along. You have gathered the information needed to create a concise plan that addresses exactly what you need to do.

When my "real" job was working as an emergency management planner, I spent my days writing, reviewing, and exercising state government plans for emergency response and recovery. I have used these plans numerous times in a variety of major disasters.

Let me just say, that while I believe in planning, the process used to create a plan is much more important (all this talking and thinking you had to do to get here). When the poo starts to fly, carefully crafted plans seem to follow it right out the window.

If you could plan and prepare for an event, and have everything in place and ready to go then it the event, by definition, is not a disaster. By the very nature of disaster, the things we prepare for are fluid and defy our attempts to prepare. That is why mindset, skills, and the ability to be flexible in our use of stuff are so important.

I took a firearm class once, where I was introduced to the idea that when your brain believes it is about to die it will desperately search for solutions. First it looks in its mental filing cabinet for things it has done, then things it has seen, and then things it has thought about, read about, and trained for. Since things you have done are stored visually, they the quickest things to assess. That is why you hear of someone's "life flashing before their eyes," its the ancient survival part of your brain trying to figure out how to save your life.

What the planning process does is to fill that cabinet up with ideas.

Questions you should address while writing in your plan may include:

- What constitutes a disaster?
- When should you dig out your emergency supplies?
- What would cause you to evacuate your house?
- Where would you go
- How would you get there
- What would you take with you?
- What sorts of medications do you need to store?
- If you have defensive concerns; what would cause me to take a life?
- What happens if an emergency occurs during the week and no one is home?
- How would you get water, food, and power during an extended emergency?

- How would you deal with sanitation during an extended period without infrastructure?
- How tightly do you want to hold the information that you have some level of preparedness?
- How would you deal with hungry neighbors that did not prepare?
- How much do you need to store
- How will you fit it all in your home?

These questions are endless, and it seems the more I answer the more questions I find to answer. It is your plan, and it is based upon your lifestyle and needs. Don't overcomplicate it, but the deeper you go the better your plan will be.

CREATE A BUDGET

Now that you know what you are planning for, what need, what you have, and how much you can spend to make those two the same. Now what you need to do is write it down into a prepper budget.

I don't get overly complicated in mine (the wife rolls her eyes at that), I just have a monthly goals I want to accomplish. This month's goal may be to buy "X" dollars of bulk food, build something, or read so many books.

Without written goals I tend to procrastinate or waste resources on pet projects that really aren't all that effective. I see this quite often with new preppers, and I did it myself. We tend to focus on really neat ideas that really aren't effective or efficient uses of our time.

These goals are time based and lead down a clear path in the direction of where I want to be.

Your goals and mine are different. I am more into **prep-steading**, and don't feel that I will ever be prepared enough until I have some acreage and the ability to grow my own crops. For almost everyone else a year's supply of food is probably more than enough.

No matter who you are, and where you want to take your desire to be more prepared for disaster, please realize that it takes action on your part. You have to get out and do it.

Writing down time based goals that complement your written plan and fit within the resource allocations you have previously made is an essential part of the process.

In the end it is all about how you manage time, money, and effort is the attempt to meet your goals.

BUILD AN IMPORTANT DOCUMENTS BINDER

I believe that prepping is a lifestyle, and that the actions you take to prepare for disaster ought to make your life easier. For the beginning prepper, nothing illustrates this more than an emergency document binder.

All this binder does is organize and store your vital identity documents and other paperwork. If you buy a sturdy binder and some clear plastic sheet protectors and business card sheets you can collect your birth certificates, social security cards, insurance paperwork, licenses, marriage and divorce documentation, voter registration, mortgage paperwork, and whatever other documents that you may need at a moment's notice.

This makes your day to day life easier, as you don't have to search for records when you need them, but in a situation where you have to leave quickly having everything in one place is the difference between the relief of having the documents you need with you and having added the stress of having to replace everything.

As with all things prepping, you can go as deep with this as you want. I found DVD sleeves that attach to binders with adhesive, and have begun putting DVD copies of my course material in my training binders. I can see the benefit of putting PDF copies of your documents, scans of your medical records, and digital copies of your irreplaceable family photos.

Keeping your important documents together is just good common sense

While working with evacuees for hurricane Katrina and Gustav, it came to my attention that many in the shelters did not have their identity documents because they were lost during the storm and resulting chaos. While case manager's helped them replace the paperwork. I am sure that the citizen's did not need the extra difficulty of having to do that.

Prepping should make life easier, and this binder is the first step of realizing that.

ORGANIZE A 72 HOUR KIT

Every website on disaster preparedness, from Government website like **FEMA** and **Ready.gov**, to nongovernmental websites like the **Red Cross**, or prepper sites like **mine**, has a section on organizing a 72 hour kit.

The reason for this is simple, if you can take care of yourself for three days without needing outside assistance, you can weather the vast majority of situations. For large-scale disasters, it will take at least three days for the governmental response agencies to get their systems activated and in place.

During the Nashville floods of 2010, the State of Tennessee began ordering vital supplies immediately, but it took time to load the trucks and drive them in from neighboring states. Everything then need to be o loaded and sent to points of distribution to be given to needed citizens. In large-scale disasters, local responders might also be victims themselves.

It is just common sense to take such universal advice. So what should you put in your kit?

An example of a small 72-hour kit

Obviously you need 72 hours' worth of food and water, but what kind and how much. Personally, I don't use military based MREs for my long term food storage. They are too expensive, have too short of a shelf life, and when I was in the Marines I ate my ll of them. However, the convenience of them outweighs the negatives for short-term kits. They are very portable and contain enough calories that 2 MREs a day can keep you going. That means a $60 pack of 12 meals would last a family of 4 for 3 days.

Add the recommended 1 gallon a day per person allowance of water, and a 6 gallon water tote makes up a great start.

I have a pair of spare eyeglasses and prescription medicine in my kit, as well as some wool blankets, a non-electric can opener, lots of garbage bags, flashlights, batteries, and anything else I would need to get my family through three long days.

A NEW PACK OF CARDS, a Hoyle card game rulebook, and some coloring books are also vital to your sanity. The iPods probably won't have juice enough to last through a minor disaster, and kids need to have something to do to prevent meltdowns.

This isn't a pack it and forget it kit, you need to check the contents a couple times a year and rotate the food and batteries.

If you never check it, then the odds are that the gear will be broken, missing, or expired when it is time to actually use it.

MAKE A COMMUNICATIONS PLAN

We are a society that is built upon our communications infrastructure. We commute long distances to work, and rely very heavily on our cellular phones to conduct business.

Since our networks are built in response to demand, it is very easy to overtax the system. If you have ever noticed that you get more dropped cell calls during rush hour you can easily extrapolate that during crisis it is very likely that cell service will be inoperable.

However, that is not the only means to communicate. If you have a cell phone and can send SMS text messages, you may have better luck with them because texts use less data than a voice call, and your phone can hold it until it can find enough available bandwidth to get the message out.

Also, certain phone companies have mentioned that due to the way the system is designed calls outside of affected areas can get through when calls within disaster areas are blocked.

During the Alabama tornadoes of 2011, I was able to use my

cell phone to call my wife's family and pass messages back and forth when they could not call each other directly even though they were only a few miles apart.

Having a communications plan is more than deciding to become a ham radio operator (even though that is a good idea, and not as hard as many think).

Part of a communications plan is bout about actions like establishing an out of state contact person that can relay messages, and partly about learning what you can do to communicate during a disaster.

An example might be that you and your wife both commute to work, and your jobs and your home are in three separate counties. If you have a large disaster during the workweek, and you cannot communicate via normal channels, you will both head home. You may decide that if your wife does not come home within a specified time frame you will go to her, and that she could leave a special mark on her route to designate she took an alternate route so you do not search in the wrong area.

This could also be a nonverbal signal that you can use in public to signal danger. In my firearm classes we go over the idea that you really don't want to be in a gunfight, but you REALLY don't want to be in one with the wife walking next to hugged up on your dominant hand. Maybe a signal to take the kids and "go away" might be worth talking about...

CREATE A PLAN TO "BUG-OUT"

In the disaster preparedness world, there are a few main schools of thought about "bugging out," some do it as a first resort, others as a last resort, and some live full time at their bug-out locations because they already own a homestead.

I don't have any hard and fast rules about bugging out or hunkering down. I personally feel that as long as it is safe to do so, I would rather stay at home because I have a lot more resources at home than I can carry on my back. Besides that, once you leave your home during a disaster, you may not be able to come back; you also may not be able to get to where you were planning to go.

However, my house is not my primary focus, and all the stuff in it is only there for the benefit of my family. If the situation called for leaving, I would leave in a heartbeat. I would not want to disregard an evacuation order and hope a National Guard helicopter would rescue us from the top of our roof.

However, I don't want to leave the relative security of my home without a plan.

When I step up my long-term food storage, I do so in a way that my food is split up into functional areas. Instead of packing one 5 gallon bucket full of wheat, I take that same bucket and put smaller bags in it, so that I would have 2 gallons of wheat, one of salt, sugar, and beans. That way if I had to leave and did not have the time to sort through buckets I could grab a couple and not have to worry about accidentally grabbing a bucket of baking powder, and another of salt.

I also have some large plastic bins that have the basic function marked on them with colored duct tape. Red is medical, green is camping supplies, white is defensive items, and blue is food. I don't have to waste time searching for stuff; I can just fill the truck up with one each if I only had a few minutes to prepare to leave.

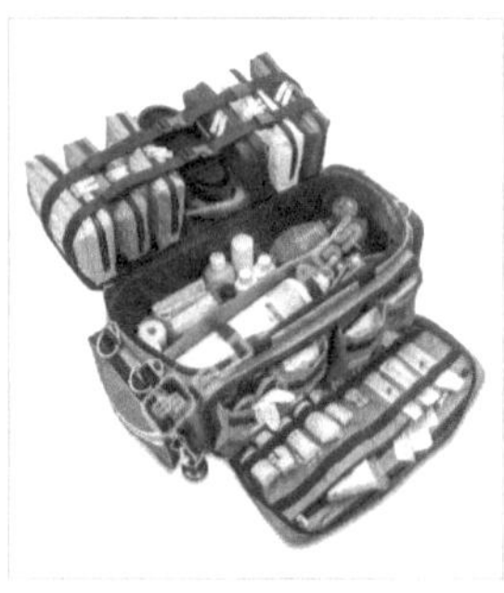

Color coding gear makes it much easier to find

Not only does your plan need to address what to take, but also it needs to cover where to go and how to get there. I hate it when non-preppers tell me they are coming to my house in the event of a disaster, and I am touchy about doing that to my friends. I have agreements with a few close friends and family that I can go to their house, and they can come to mine in the event of a disaster. Some are local, others regional, and a few are out of state.

I have looked at maps to find alternative routes to their

homes, and when time is available I try to run those routes in advance and look for places to rest and refuel on the way.

The last thing I can tell you about bugging out is, that if you think you may have to, it is best to be the first one out. If you wait too long, you may find the road is impassable.

13

BUILD A "BUG OUT BAG"

A bug out bag is not the same as a 72-hour kit; it can be larger if designed for a car, or smaller if it designed to be used as a backpack. I have tried both over the years and have compromised to find a solution that works best for me.

What I did was stock more items in a large plastic tote, and include a backpack. I keep this kit in my car and if I should ever have to walk home or had to leave the house with no notice I can pick and choose from the car kit and put the items in the backpack.

Alternatively, if you did not want to fill up your car with a kit, you could build a kit around a backpack and keep it stored somewhere in your home that is easy to access, but out of the way. It would be nice if it was not hidden away so that you forget to rotate your food and expendable gear, but if it is too accessible, I find that it becomes an easy place to raid for batteries when the TV remote dies, or the kid wants a granola bar.

I will caution you about the outward appearance of your kit. As I watch YouTube and visit prepper related sites, I see a lot of folks with military looking gear. I would not be very accommodating if, during a large-scale disaster, a couple armed men with chest rigs and camouflage packs strolled through my yard. (However, it is pretty normal here where I live.)

Depending on the situation, I can see several bad endings, from arrest to being killed for your stuff.

My pack is a beat up looking, but is in good condition. It is a nice and dirty looking dark blue. If the situation called for it, and I choose to carry a gun in the kit, it would probably not be a military caliber rifle. I think they have a definite place in disaster preparations, but in most of the situations I can think of that have a realistic chance of occurring, it is my opinion that they bring too much negative attention for the benefits they bring. (For bugging out and walking down the road that is.)

Remember, the military uses firepower for suppression, and are just a radio call from resupply.

If you have ever tried carrying 300 rounds of ammo and a rifle in addition to your kit, you will find that it cuts down on maneuverability. However, a nice sized handgun, concealed about your person, while looking non-threatening but alert, and without any ostentatious gear screaming, "Rob Me!" may be a better solution.

It is not about looking cool, or feeling like John Wayne, it is about getting to safety as quickly and efficiently as possible.

14

STORE WATER AND LEARN TO PURIFY IT

Earlier, when discussing 72-hour kits I mentioned that the standard amount of water recommended is one gallon per person per day. This is a universal recommendation, but depending on time of year, climate, and if you want to stay clean, it is not enough. However, when balancing the weight and size of water, with its universal use, one gallon a day is a good compromise.

We store water in a variety of ways both for utility, for redundancy, and for convenience. Our main method of storing water is to use plastic 5-gallon jerry cans. They used to sell these at Wal-Mart for around $10, but I haven't seen one there in 10 years. I have seen them at sporting good stores for $20, and I have a standing order with the wife to buy any she sees, whenever she finds them if they are $20 or less.

Right now I keep 5 full of water next to the washer in out basement. I consider that a 4 day supply for the kid, my wife, and I. That gives me some extra to take care of hygiene.

I also try to take clear 2 liter soda bottles, and after cleaning out the soda, refill them, and freeze them in our deep freezer. The machine is more efficient when full, and if the power is out for a short time, the ice acts to moderate the temperature.

Whatever method of storage you use, make sure you add a little chlorine to the bottle to kill any pathogens.

Use non-scented chlorine bleach, and only add a few drops per gallon. The chlorine will dissipate over time, but if sealed tightly, no bacteria can get in.

Like food, you cannot store enough water to survive long term;

You need to have a method to get water if the electricity is down. I keep extra food grade buckets to transfer water from a nearby creek.

I also have several methods of purifying the water. Boiling works well, but it takes a lot of energy, filters also work well, and I have several but they may not filter out all the pathogens. I have a bulk container of chorine based powder pool-shock that I can use to make a bleach solution to add to the water to kill bacteria.

This is one area where you cannot skimp, water purification methods are too cheap, too plentiful, and the risks from drinking unsafe water too great to risk not taking the extra step.

Water borne diarrhea is uncomfortable during normal times, but is a major cause of death in countries without infrastructure, in crisis, or otherwise lacking medical facilities.

STORE FOOD AND ROTATE IT

With the exception of rearms, nothing in the world of personal preparedness has as many differing viewpoints of what is "the right way" as food storage. What to store, how much to store, and how to store the food are all things you will have to decide for yourself. There are a few different routes you can take based upon your resources and concerns.

The first thing you have to decide is what your target amount of food to store is. 3 days of food for your family is the universally recommended starting point, but consider how short a time that is. There have been many winter storms that have impacted communities for twice or three times the 72-hour number. A pandemic u could have an incubation period of a week, and to prevent exposure you may have to stay sheltered in your home for 10 or more days.

We have a target of one year for the three people in my household. However, I have several family members who may come to my house during a disaster. If that occurs, my 3 person year supply turns to a 6 month supply with 6 people, or much shorter supply if my parents come and my sister brings her 6 kids.

Once you decide on a target amount, you need to decide are you going to pack the food yourself or are you going to buy it commercially. I have bought 50# bags of wheat for under $15, but a 44# bucket of wheat packaged for storage can cost $50.00. Time is valuable, and there is a learning curve to packing your own, but the cost savings can be tremendous.

What types of food to store is also a decision point. We use the LDS guidelines of 400 pounds of grain, 60 pounds of beans, 16 pounds milk (triple if you have kids), 10 quarts cooking oil, 60 pounds sugar or honey, and 8 pounds salt per person.

This will keep you alive, is cheap, and when packed and stored properly it can last a lifetime. However it is not the most fun diet in the world.

To help with food fatigue, we augmenting it with foods we NORMALLY eat. This adds variety as well as keep incorporate our food storage into our daily life to both adjust our bodies to the food, and to learn how to cook it in enjoyable ways You can buy freeze dried bulk food also, and I recommend doing so if your budget allows. It stores well, gives variety to your meals, and tastes much better than sprouted wheat and powdered milk. Unfortunately it is much more expensive, and many of the prepackaged deals that advertise a certain amount of calories per day pad their numbers with a lot of wheat at inflated costs.

MRE's and other shelf stable convenience meals are also useful, but they don't last as long, are more bulky, and cost the most of any of the other options. However, for short-term disasters the convenience offered can offset the negative aspects.

The key is to test the items you store so you pick things that you will eat and enjoy, and then incorporate these items into your daily life so that you are eating what you store, and storing what you eat, this helps keep your inventory fresh, as well as keeping your body from having a huge shock due to a change in diet.

16

CONSIDER DEFENSIVE STRATEGIES

The most controversial subject in prepping has to be guns. I am not going to get into the politics of gun ownership, and this is too short a space to delve too deep into training. There are three things I want to emphasize that are vitally important to a prepper.

There are "preppers" (and you may be one of them), that foresees a coming disaster that will be catastrophic, and they choose to prepare for it. However, these "preppers" chose to prepare in one solitary aspect. They buy guns.

If your disaster preparedness plans are all about guns and have nothing about food, you are not prepping, you are planning to murder people for their food.

You are saying when the "shit hits the fan" you are going to go out and steal from people who have food. If you go the opposite route and have no defensive tools then you are planning to become a victim.

Guns are tools, and not objects of worship. I like guns, I like that they represent equality and freedom, and I enjoy shooting them, but I don't buy them for looks, or to be cool. I buy rearms with a proven track record in common calibers. My collection won't impress my friends, and are not the newest gun featured in a magazine, but they go bang every time I pull the trigger, and shoot calibers that are common enough to be found in any sporting goods store.

Owning a gun does not mean you know to use it effectively. Shooting is a skill, not a gift. You have to practice and you have to have some degree of academic knowledge.

You do not have to spend a fortune and go to fancy shooting schools, but proper training from a skilled instructor is well worth the effort.

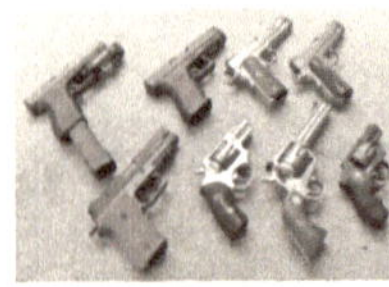

Get the best you can afford

As a firearm instructor I have seen the difference quality makes when it comes to guns and accessories. I know that everyone cannot afford a new gun, and that any gun is better than no gun. But when students come to a class and have an extremely inexpensive gun that has not been properly taken care of, a gun that malfunctions often rewards them for their choices.

Nothing is louder than a click when you need a bang. On the other side of the coin, I see students bring in very expensive guns and try to shoot cheap bullets and carry the gun on a cheap belt in a cheaper holster. They spend an inordinate amount of time fumbling around with an uncomfortable setup.

As a new prepper, if you are serious about wanting to own a gun, I would take some simple steps. First I would take a basic class. The NRA, or a state carry permit class (if available) are perfect class choices for new shooters.

Then I would find a range that rents guns and shoot several different types of guns to get a feel for what you think is comfortable. I would then buy a gun, bullets, and if a pistol a holster and belt, that are good enough quality that you can afford them, but is expensive enough that you feel it.

You need something that is quality so that it is reliable, large enough so that it moderates the recoil of the cartridge, and the largest cartridge you are comfortable with.

Gun ownership is a personal issue, and I am hesitant to recommend a particular model over another without knowing a person's circumstances, but a decent pistol in 9mm, .38, .40, or .45 works well, as do shotguns in 12 or 20 gauge, and rifles in common calibers such as .223, .308, or 30-06.

17

DON'T FORGET LIGHTING

In most disasters that someone could reasonably plan for, it is a good assumption that the power grid will be down. Electrical power can be an issue, but once you realize that electrical power is relatively new and that people have survived thousands of years without it, you should realize that you could survive without it also.

That being said, the things that electricity powers are important, and lighting is something you definitely need to be prepared. If you cannot find your circuit breaker in the dark because you don't have batteries in your flashlight then you are a very poor prepper. Like all things related to preparedness, we follow the tiered approach, and are as redundant as possible.

I have a habit of buying small led flashlights and hanging them on the backs of bedroom doorknobs. They are out of the way, very handy, and by being inside of bedrooms; they do not interfere with my wife's decorating scheme. The LED flashlights are very handy, and do not take a lot of power to work, so a stockpile of AA batteries can last a long time.

We keep a high-intensity "tactical" light in the bedroom, as well as a lower power, but more efficient D-cell mag-light.

I have several camping lanterns, fuel, and mantles in my camping boxes, as well as old style kerosene lamps and lots of candles. However, if you are going to rely on flammable lighting, matches, wicks, fuel, fire protection, and smoke and CO alarms are mandatory to store also.

simple mason jar oil lamp

I have learned how to make my own candles and make simple lamps from **mason jars**, cotton strung, wire, and old olive oil. Simply bend a wire (or paperclip) to hold a bit of cotton string right at the surface level of oil in a jar. The cotton will wick up the oil and burn with little smoke and is relatively bright.

However, since the majority of our lighting comes from flash-lights, we store lots of batteries. I prefer rechargeable batteries, and have a small solar charger. They are more expensive, but are more economical with use.

18

TEST YOUR PLAN, GEAR, & YOURSELF

I commend you for recognizing the need to become more prepared, and if you have taken the steps to get you to this point you now have a plan of action as well as the basic ability to support yourself with food, water, light, and keep people from stealing your food water and light the next thing to do is to test your plan.

Without actually testing your plan you have no idea that it can work, not only that, but by testing it you push your prepping skills higher up that mental toolbox so that if you are ever unexpectedly thrown into disaster your mind has a stronger frame of reference. That will allow you to better manage the stress as well as to react quicker.

There is a science to exercising plans, you don't go all out and kill your electricity and try to survive for a month the first time out. Professional emergency managers work up to full-scale exercises by first having what is known as a table top.

In a tabletop exercise, all the key players sit down at a table and are presented with a problem. For example, a tornado came through town and your home was not destroyed, but the roof was damaged, and power is out. Each player will then say what they would do based upon what they have, not what they want. The key is to only use skills, knowledge, and equipment you have available. This will help identify what else you need.

A family camping trip is also a great way to test a 72-hour or bug out kit

Once you have done that, pick a weekend when everyone is home, and commit to having a trial run without using your utilities. That means no electricity, no heat or cooling, and no running water.

Use only what you have at your house, and set up a schedule so that someone is always awake during the night to be on " fire watch".

It's not particularly fun, but it is an invaluable training tool to help you realize that you can survive hardship, as well as help you gain experience in what works and what does not.

19

CONDUCT AN AFTER-ACTION MEETING

Immediately after an exercise, professional responders frequently have what is known as a "hot wash" or after action briefing. No matter what you call it, this gives emergency personnel the opportunity to discuss what works, what doesn't and how to improve.

It is vital that you do this at the end of your weekend exercise before everyone gets back on their iPad and returns to normal life.

Make sure that no matter what happened in your trial run, the discussion stays positive. If junior snuck in the kitchen and ate all the survival cookies, don't say,"junior ate all the cookies". Point out that maybe you need to focus on storing more food because your allotment isn't enough to satisfy, or that the fire-watch needs to be more than one person. Maybe the solution is to put a lock on the cookies? Remember the reason for an after action review it to look for solutions to problems, not people to blame.

You do not have to make this extremely formal, and it should not take a long time. However, if you wait to do it, chances are you will keep putting it off and valuable lessons will be lost.

Additionally, by planning, having a table top, having a functional exercise, and then critiquing it afterwards your brain will be "tricked" into thinking it has been involved in that type of action several times, so that if the time comes it will seem much more normal to your subconscious. That will allow you to get up to speed much more quickly.

20

REASSESS AND REPEAT

After your hot wash, both the after-action brief, and the long shower you will enjoy after the weekend with no power, begin the process of taking what you have learned and reassess you plan. What you have learned will give you insight into making a better plan. Emergency management is a cyclical discipline, and professional emergency planners are always planning, training, testing, and planning some more.

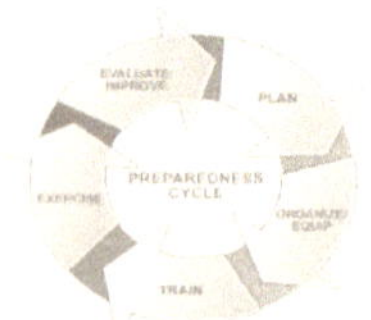

Emergency
Preparedness Cycle

Each cycle gets you more prepared for disasters, teaches your family to work as a group, and increases your comfort level.

Depending on your situation, what you are preparing for, and your level of comfort you can take this as seriously as you want. But, a single rotation of the preparedness cycle is a vast improvement over the general population.

If you keep the cycle going, and are creative in your exercises, (say exploring alternate routes of travel during a weekend getaway) you can make this a fun part of your lifestyle.

We like to take classes, and spend our time building and creating new things that make us more prepared and self-reliant, but that's because we enjoy doing it.

We prepare because we love out family, lets make it a family activity

Prepping should not be a chore; it should be a path that balances your life. Your take extra effort in easy times so you will make tough times easier.

BUILDING A GET HOME BAG

Tips for Setting Up a Realistic Bug Out Bag for Getting Back Home in a Disaster

DAVID NASH

1

INTRODUCTION

Abugout bag/72 hour kit is one of the very first projects a new prepper makes as they explore the idea of becoming more self-reliant. A quick search for the term "bug out bag" on Amazon kindle shows more than 9 pages of books. Why should you read this one?

I can only explain why by telling you my own personal ideas on the subject. With very few exceptions, the "experts" in prepping are all just selling you their own ideas and personal bias. Most of us teach what we believe, but are not a lot of writers in this subject that have lived through a grid down or other catastrophic disaster, so as I said, its all personal ideas.

I am no different, however, I have a unique set of skills. I have been a personal preparedness advocate since I led a school-wide new Madrid preparation program as a High School Freshman. After the Marines, and a few years working inside various state prisons, I began working in state level emergency management. I have a degree in Emergency Management, and worked for over a decade in preparedness planning, training, and operations at the State level. I know exactly how the government will react and what they are prepared to do. I also understand the prepper mindset, as I have been one since junior high school.

This book is similar in scope to my 21 Days to Basic Preparedness[1] ebook in that it explores personal preparations from the viewpoint of the modern science of emergency management. In this short work I will discuss the fundamental differences in types of emergency kits and bags. However, this work focuses on the specifics of a Get Home Bag rather than a more general bug out bag and why many people have this essential piece of gear built dangerously incorrect.

I have worked in emergency management during some very serious disasters. From that experience, I know the work and thought that goes into running a shelter during a disaster. Emergency management workers try very hard to make shelters safe and comfortable. However, the lack of privacy, resources, and independence makes me pretty hesitant to choose to go to a shelter as long as I have other options.

Personally, it would take a very severe reason for me to evacuate or "bug out" from my home in the first place. Leaving the house would entail me having to leave many of my in-place systems and make me more vulnerable to outlaws and well meaning (and otherwise) bureaucrats.

However, just because I don't WANT to evacuate from my homestead doesn't mean I won't HAVE to evacuate. I don't want any kind of disaster to befall my family, but measuring risk says I should be prepared "just in case".

While, my goal is to not have to bug out, I can see lots of situations where I would need to "get home"

Before we get into the necessity to have a special kit in your vehicle that will help you "get home". There is a need to discuss the various types of emergency kits. However, buying a bag of stuff won't help if you don't have the skills and mindset to use them. In my experience, both as a prepper, and an emergency manager, I find that before you should buy things you should develop the right skills.

PERSONAL PREPAREDNESS MINDSET

P ersonal preparedness means different things depending on who you are and what your situation is. To an inhabitant of the Florida Keys, preparedness means having items to outlast a hurricane. To a city dweller, preparedness might be having a can of mace in her purse. To a survivalist, preparedness might mean having a semi trailer loaded with M14 rifles buried in the back yard. Depending on the situation, any of these definitions might be appropriate. Whatever your situation, cultivating a personal preparedness mindset is the key to thriving in times of adversity.

Personal preparedness is simply knowing what dangers are likely to befall you and taking reasonable precautions to avoid or survive them. In today's modern world, insurance is a required item. No one laughs at a car owner that buys a full coverage policy for his or her car. As a matter of fact, a driver that fails to insure their car is looked upon as irresponsible, sometimes even criminal. The same thing can be said about homeowner's or renter's insurance, life insurance, and health insurance. Today people take out money for retirement in the form of IRA's, 401K's, mutual funds and the like. No one faults them. Why is it then that someone who has a pantry of stored food, candles, a rifle or two, and ammunition for them is considered crazy or dangerous? Isn't it a logical extension of the doctrine of insurance? After all insurance is merely a device to lessen the extent a disaster has on your life. If having an extra insurance policy for break-ins is smart, then the idea of someone breaking into your home is possible. If it is likely that someone might break into your home, then having a means to protect yourself is justified.

Each year natural disasters occur in the United States. When these occur, the news media rushes to the scene. It never fails that they show a relief organization van at the disaster site. Usually there is an interview with someone who is standing in line looking for help. The site is common; a desperate parent with a hungry child waiting for someone to give them some milk for their infant. Ratings soar and people feel sorry for this poor child. Consider this, areas prone to natural disaster are known. Floods happen on a regular basis. Places like Tornado Alley have been recognized and named. If the choice is made to live in an area like this and the basic precautions are not taken, then pity is not the logical emotion. Irresponsibility on the part of the parent caused the child's pain; it only takes a few extra seconds to grab a couple extra bottles of formula. Why didn't they take this simple precaution? They probably paid the cable bill. Does that expense outweigh the measly cost of a gallon of Bottled water?

Organizations like the American Red Cross and the Office of Homeland Security suggest that each family have a few days of essential items[1] to get them through an emergency. Doing this is not hard nor does it have to be expensive. No one says that preparedness means having a years supply of freeze dried steak in a concrete storage bunker. Simply buying a can or two of extra food every time you go shopping is enough. Buy an extra box of garbage bags, some extra toilet tissue, or any item you have to have. Store it in a box under the bed, or in the closet. In hardly any time at all, you will soon have a store pile that will give you not only an added measure of security, but also a sense of well-being. Rotate this stock out. As you eat a box of macaroni, buy another. Forget that you have four boxes on your kitchen shelf. This causes you not to feel over burdened financially to support your prepared lifestyle. It also keeps your store fresh. An added benefit is that your safety net is familiar to you. In the stressful time of disaster, you don't have the added stressor of eating unfamiliar foods chosen not by your appetite, but by their shelf life.

It is easy to lecture on what items are needed. Lists of essential items depend on lifestyle and location as much as physical needs. It would be irresponsible to dictate what equipment your family would need to survive without knowing you or your situation. You must sit down and decide what your family's priorities are, and from that list correlate your family's needs.

It is not important what others say or think of you. It is not even recommended to tell your neighbors you find the need to be prepared for life. Does it matter if they think you are crazy for stocking up added groceries? Will it matter if your children or spouse suffer because you want to keep the good graces of the people 2 doors down?

3

TYPES OF EMERGENCY KITS

Any prepper or interested party with access to the internet has probably noticed the love of acronyms as they relate to kits and gear. You have: BOB, INCH, GOOD, GHB, and EDC, IFAK, 72 hour kits, and 1st 2nd and 3rd line gear. The confusion just piles on.

Basically, it all related to the stuff you need to survive and the philosophy that caused you to pack it all together.

Back during my podcasting days, one of my most popular episodes dealt with an introduction to prepper kits[1].

Basically it all starts with the 72 hour kit, which comes from the US military and is based around the fact that American soldiers are resupplied so often that they only need to be self-sufficient for three days at a time. This level is what the US government recommends for all citizens, because in the event of a federally declared disaster it will take FEMA approximately three days to get a supply system organized to provide relief. A 72 hour kit should have basic cooking, lighting, shelter, water, and food to survive for three days.

Everyday Carry

EDC or everyday carry are things you have on you everyday. A whole prepper subset has evolved around EDC. Generally for me my EDC is a couple knives, a cell phone, a cheap screwdriver set and P-38 on my key chain, and if I am carrying my "man purse" I'll have some Altoid tins containing a sewing kit and OTC medicine, and some car charger adaptors. I would love to have a pistol in my EDC, but I work at a prison so that is verboten.

Bug Out Bag

BOB, bob, or B.o.B means Bug Out Bag. A BOB is a small bag that is basically a portable 72 hour kit. The idea is that if a fire or something broke out and you had to leave RIGHT NOW, you can throw on your shoes, grab your BOB and have whatever essential medicines, food, and clothes that you would need. A good idea is to have copies of vital records in your bob, so that you won't lose them if you don't have time to dig around in your filing cabinet.

Get Out of Dodge Bag

A GOOD bag or Get out of Dodge bag, is a larger BOB, but still small enough to pack quickly. It's pretty much inter-changeable with a BOB. Some preppers have GOOD trailers or GOOD vehicles that are pre-packed. I use big plastic totes with a color code system. Each food tote contains approximately a month of food rather than a single commodity. In an emergency I can grab as many as I have room for and not have to worry about grabbing a 50 pound bucket of wheat but forgetting the salt or grinder.

I'm Never Coming Home Bag

An INCH bag on the other hand means "I'm Never Coming Home". Its more of a Mad Max/The Road/Postman type problem where you have to take what you can carry, but all you get it what you take. My inch bag would contain everything in my GOOD kit, plus extras like my hand reloading press, more tools, and reference materials.

Individual First Aid Kit / Improved First Aid Kit

IFAK is not a general preparedness kit, but it took me a minute to connect the dots so I will throw it in as a "good to know" IFAK is an improved first aid kit. This improved kit that is part of a new military Soldier in a system initiative. It basically is a one pound kit that addresses major blood loss and airway distress.

Line Gear

Line gear is also a military concept and revolves around the gear you would need to complete a mission. It's not exactly applicable to citizen preppers, but it is related in many ways.

First Line Gear is your EDC, and focuses on what you would carry on your person. This would include your clothing, knife, weapon and maybe a small survival and first aid kit. Obviously, if you're a office worker your EDC would be much different from a law enforcement officer, or a coal miner. Don't go mall ninja on me though and carry a bunch of neato jiffy wow stuff to feel cool. Everything needs a use or you won't carry it all the time.'

2nd line gear is your "fighting load". When I have my "jack baur bag" (my wife calls it a "murse" but jack pack, messenger bag are all appropriate terms.) I can carry more prepper stuff, flashlights, hand held radio, batteries, power bars. It also can go with me almost everywhere and gives me more capability without sacrificing a lot of maneuverability. IF it was a full on WROL (without rule of law, IMHO that is VERY unlikely) this would most likely take the form of a load bearing vest, or chest rig to hold ammunition for your rifle.

3rd line gear is your pack, i.e. sustainment items you need for a longer term. Your not going to fight wearing your rucksack, you would drop it and depend on your 1st and 2nd line gear during the fight and then go back and get your pack to refill your empty magazines.

The thing is, who cares what you call your stuff, organize it to suit your needs and as long as you understand what your doing and why you are light years ahead of guys that follow the conventional prepper wisdom and build kits based upon what some internet guru wrote in a list. Your also Galaxies ahead of people that don't even have a thought about prepping.

You don't need to be scared, but it is important that you take some time to develop a plan that you can work with.

4

WHAT IS A GET HOME BAG

GHB or Get Home Bag is practically the same as a BOB, but philosophically the opposite. A GHB is a portable kit containing the essentials you would need if you have to find an alternate route home if disaster struck while you were away from home. I work at a local prison, that is a 45 minute drive from my home. My wife teaches at a school 45 minutes in the opposite direction. If something were to happen during the work day we are three counties apart. How would we be able to survive, to communicate, and to get home?

If something happened and I had to leave my car and walk home, I would want a light backpack type kit that allowed me to change out of my work clothes, and gave me some comfort and security on a long trek home. I keep a GHB in both mine, and my wife's vehiclesBecause the Get Home Bag sits in a car trunk, weight is not an issue, and space is not a substantially limiting factor. However, if I have to carry the kit on my back, then weight and space mist definitely is. As backpackers and soldiers know; ounces make pounds, pounds make pain.

What I do, is keep a box with lots of related items in the trunks of the cars. Then, in a disaster, I can sort through and pick what is needed for the specifics of the event.

Space and weight is not an issue in the car, so I have things in my box that I can pick through to make a bag that best fits my situation. In many ways my GHB is actually a box that has items for light vehicle repair, minimalist camping, and t0 expedite a walk home.

Don't misunderstand, in a disaster, I am not going to have time to unload and pack a bag for scratch. I keep the essentials in a small day pack, and have items like a car survival/emergency kit with jumper cables, 12 volt air pump, LED road flares and spare tools.

Car Emergency Kits

Car survival kits are specifically designed to provide survival supplies if you are trapped in or become disabled or lost in your vehicle. Automobile emergency kits are not the same as a Survival kit. An automobile kit generally contain flares, jumper cables, spare fuses, etc. They help the car, not you.

Most folks don't understand why a car kit is important. However, those same people can vividly recall the news reports of a person pinned in their wrecked car for days.

5

THE REALITY OF A GET HOME BAG

True story:

The prison I work at had a random car search, and the shift "mall ninja" had to open up his car. In the back of the car they found a moss berg 590 12 gauge shotgun with the breeching barrel. Why would an employee at a prison have a shotgun in his car designed to blow hinges off doors? When asked he said it was part of his "get home kit" in the event he had to walk home. Under the shotgun was a plate carrier and chest rig to carry the spare magazines he had for the semi-automatic AK-47 clone he had stashed under the bullet proof vest. Once again, it was part of his get home kit. He also had a Glock pistol, a military molle pack, a cold steel ninja sword, a tomahawk, and 1000 rounds of various ammunition.

Looking past the size and shape of the individual and my belief he couldn't carry all his equipment a mile, much less all the way home. I am a big out of shape guy myself, so don't think I am fat shaming, but consider that a thousand rounds of anything, including .22 long rifle is heavy. So are the guns.

Besides the weight, what would you do during a disaster if you saw a corn fed crisco kid dressed out in military camouflage, carrying an AK and a sword walking through your subdivision in the middle of the night?

Many people keep firearms in their GHB's and I totally understand that, I do to. However, if you have a AR or AK platform long gun and change into a multi-cam uniform, you are going to attract unwanted attention. Consider a more concealable approach to defensive weaponry.

Personally, I want to look like Joe Sixpack with no more on me than anyone else. In a disaster I want to blend in until I have to stand out. Chances are, you know someone that would shoot him and take his stuff. On top of all that, I *know* what a law enforcement official will do when spotting Paul Blart toting his arsenal during a declared State of Emergency

You Can't Carry Everything

The reality is, ounces make pounds, pounds make pain. You are not backpacking the Sierra Nevada Mountains, nor are you out on a long range reconnaissance patrol. The role of a get home bag is to be light, fast, unobtrusive, and contain only what you need to support a fast trek home.

My GHB is stashed in a sturdy, yet older blue school book bag. On the surface it is beat up, yet it is well made. It contains items similar to what an ultra light backpacker would carry. I am not looking for comfort, I am looking for a kit to be comforting. A change of clothes that I can walk in, yet look unthreatening, broke in boots and thick socks, a pistol and 50 or so rounds in a good quality concealment holster, some food, water, and comms gear.

Unless forced, I don't plan on fighting anyone, my goal is to avoid trouble on my way home. To be honest, I don't really plan on sleeping much or doing anything more than getting home as fast as and efficiently as possible. How could I, if I have to walk home, I would be separated from my wife and son in a major disaster.

A Trunk is Not Always the Best Place for a Kit

Your supplies may be inaccessible in your trunk if you are actually trapped in your vehicle. This depends on you vehicle. For such a scenario, you'd want supplies within reach of the passenger compartment. This may not be a problem for a minivan or SUV where there is access to the entire vehicle and you or your passengers can reach the supplies.

However, sedans with a separate trunk are trickier. You could be trapped in the driver's seat and be unable to access your supplies. Although, to be fair, a scenarios where you are trapped and can't get to your trunk have a very low probability of occurrence. Additionally, most victims are found before they need survival gear.

Although, when it is just my wife and I, I move our kit to the backseat of our car. Keeping your car survival kit in the trunk would prove effective for the majority of your scenarios. However, an extended jam could have you wishing for water.

Just think about the parking lot known as Interstate 45 from Galveston to Houston any time an evacuation order is given for a hurricane!

Hot Trunks Will Reduce Storage Life

Another major consideration is shelf life in the vehicle. Car interiors get very hot in the summer, and very cold in the winter. This can wreak havoc on the storage life of your supplies.

For this reason, I use glass bottles to store my water because I don't tolerate the BPA leached from the plastic bottle into my water very well. Leaching will occur over time from any plastic water bottle, but in a hot trunk it will occur much faster. I keep a hydration bladder in my kit, but it is empty and will be filled from the glass bottles.

I have the same issue with food. I don't dislike the lemony taste of USCG approved ration bars like the Datrex, but I don't like the flaky oatmeal texture. However, of all the emergency rations I have experimented with, they have the best shelf stability in a hot car trunk.

I keep lighters stashed everywhere, the same as in my box of GHB 'stuff', in this instance I use a zippo lighter kit stored in a ziplock bag. This is a new in box setup, that contains the lighter, flints, wick, and a can of the fluid. The fluid is volatile and will evaporate over time, so in my trunk I keep a can of the fluid and only fill my 'emergency' zippo with the fluid as I leave the car.

MUST HAVE ESSENTIALS FOR A GET HOME BAG

A get home bag is not built for comfort or long term survival. Its sole function is to get you home as quickly as possible with as little drama as possible.

As noted survivalist Mors Kochanski[1] says, "The more you know the less you carry." If you have skills, then your bag can be smaller.

Like military line gear, the things you keep on your person everyday can help you in a disaster evacuation situation. Some, like myself, work in a place that limits my every day carry items, you may not be.

Because I work in a prison, the only items I can constantly plan on having is a small P-38 military can opener on my keychain. Everything else must stay in my car. I am also limited on what can be in the car. Obviously, I cannot keep a long gun like an AR-15 in my car on prison grounds. That really is not the problem some may think it is. Earlier I mentioned why I believe typical long guns do not have a place in a basic get home bag setup.

For those that have better options for everyday carry, I set up a list of lists[2] on good everyday carry items for various types of people. I even have a list for those in non-permissive environments that don't allow weapons.

What is Important Now

I have a car kit in the event my vehicle breaks down. During normal situations, if I cannot fix it, I call my wife so she doesn't worry and I call a tow truck. I don't need much besides basic tools, and maybe some water.

If there is some type of disaster, everything changes. I need a plan, a means to get home, and a way to communicate with my wife.

Get Home Bag Content Checklist

I have a page with links[3] to various examples of items n this list, and can recommend all the items on that list as being a good value or a particularly good item.

As mentioned before, I like a modular kit, so not everything on this list is to be carried if the vehicle is left, but everything on this list has a purpose in the event you are stranded and either need to get help or walk home.

This is what I have in mine, feel free to add or delete as you find necessary

Car Recovery and Basic Repair

- Large rectangular Milk Crate

- Wool Blanket
- Watch Cap and Gloves
- Emergency Roadside Toolkit with tow strap, shovel, jumper cables, and basic tools
- Emergency LED Road Flares
- 12volt Portable Air Compressor
- Jack and 4 way lug wrench
- Come-along portable winch
- Road Atlas (preferably with topographical maps)
- Set of 4-33.75 Oz Glass Bottles with Stopper Caps filled with water
- Gallon of Oil
- 2 Gallons pre-mixed antifreeze
- Large contractor garbage bags

Basic Get Home Bag Kit

- Hydration Backpack
- 3 Day supply of Datrex 3600 Calorie Food Bars
- Camping tarp with lines and stakes
- Ultralight ground tarp
- Ultralight Sleeping Bag
- Ultralight Backpacking first aid kit
- Portable Water Filter Pump
- Titanium mug/pot
- Multi-tool
- Air Force Survival Knife
- Zippo All in One Kit
- 100 Feet Paracord
- Hooded Rain Jacket
- Emergency Headlamp
- Handheld CB radio (Marine is better, but less legal day to day)

- 100% Deet insect repellant
- Compass and maps for area
- Wool Hiking socks (2 pair)
- Good broken in Hiking boots
- Change of sturdy clothes, non-cotton.

I also keep a 9mm Glock 19 and 5 magazines in my kit, as well as a tinker model Swiss army knife and a Bic lighter in my glove compartment as well as a a mag-light.

My truck has more tools in it, my wife's car has less.

Your milage may vary, but you aren't fighting World War Three or Zombies. If you try to carry too much you will wish you had not tried to backpack with the kitchen sink.

NOTES

1. Introduction

1. https://shepherdpublish.com/self-published-works/21-days-to-basic-preparedness/

2. Personal Preparedness Mindset

1. https://www.tngun.com/completed-incremental-disaster-kit/

3. Types of Emergency Kits

1. https://www.tngun.com/prn-40-alphabet-kits/

6. Must Have Essentials for a Get Home Bag

1. https://en.wikipedia.org/wiki/Mors_Kochanski
2. https://www.tngun.com/list-of-edc-lists/
3. https://www.tngun.com/essential-gear-for-a-get-home-bag/

Introduction

1. https://www.tngun.com

1. What is Pepper Spray?

1. http://www.historyofwar.org/articles/weapons_metsubishi.html
2. https://www.smithsonianmag.com/history/forgotten-history-mace-designed-29-year-old-and-reinvented-police-weapon-180953239/

3. What is the Proper Mindset?

1. https://en.wikipedia.org/wiki/Tennessee_v._Garner
2. https://en.wikipedia.org/wiki/Graham_v._Connor
3. http://www.businessdictionary.com/definition/reasonable-person.html

5. What Type of Spray Should I Buy?

1. https://www.safariland.com/on/demandware.static/-/Sites-tsg-Library/default/dwd4ad6a29/resources/less-lethal/aerosol-reports/oc-and-pepper-sprays.pdf
2. https://www.sabrered.com/formulations-heat-strength-and-law

6. What Are the Laws on Pepper Spray?

1. https://www.atf.gov/resource-center/docs/guide/state-laws-and-published-ordinances-2010-2011-alaska/download
2. https://law.justia.com/codes/arkansas/2010/title-5/subtitle-6/chapter-73/subchapter-1/5-73-124/
3. http://consumerwiki.dca.ca.gov/wiki/index.php/Pepper_Spray_(Mace/Tear_Gas)
4. https://www.flsenate.gov/Laws/Statutes/2017/790.01
5. http://qcode.us/codes/kauaicounty/
6. http://www.legislature.mi.gov/(S(xghhgtxbpgbf2huldjzemhtk))/mileg.aspx?page=GetObject&objectname=mcl-750-224d
7. https://www.atf.gov/resource-center/docs/guide/state-laws-and-published-ordinances-2010-2011-nevada/download
8. http://codes.findlaw.com/ny/penal-law/pen-sect-265-20.html
9. http://lis.njleg.state.nj.us/nxt/gateway.dll?f=templates&fn=default.htm&vid=Publish:10.1048/Enu
10. http://apps.leg.wa.gov/RCW/default.aspx?cite=9.91.160
11. https://docs.legis.wisconsin.gov/statutes/statutes/941/III/26

10. How Do I Decontaminate Others or Myself?

1. Grossman, Dave and Loren W. Christensen. On Combat: The Psychology and Physiology of Deadly Conflict in War and Peace. 2nd ed. PPCT Research Publications, 2007

1. Introduction to Geodesic Domes

1. https://www.bfi.org/about-fuller/big-ideas/geodesic-domes
2. ttps://www.ziptiedomes.com/faq/What-Is-Geodesic-Dome-Frequency-Explained.htm
3. https://issuu.com/golfstromen/docs/lloyd-kahn-1971
4. https://www.lloydkahn.com/

2. Introduction to Ferrrocement

1. https://www.itacanet.org/ferrocement-water-tanks-and-their-construction/
2. http://adkison.name/ferro/ferro_cement_basics.html
3. https://theconstructor.org/concrete/ferrocement-in-construction/1156/
4. https://en.wikipedia.org/wiki/Ferrocement
5. ferrocement.com
6. http://ferrocement.com/intro-Ferro/intro.en.html
7. https://www.mortarsprayer.com/

3. Introduction to Latex Cement

1. https://www.researchgate.net/publication/295675998_Disposing_Waste_Latex_Paints_in_Cement-Based_Materials_-_Effect_on_Flow_and_Rheological_Properties
2. https://www.tngun.com/how-to-build-a-paintcrete-roof-outhouse/

4. Preparing EMT Conduit Spars

1. http://www.desertdomes.com/tips.html
2. http://www.domerama.com/fabricating/making-the-struts/geodesic-dome-struts-flattening/
3. http://www.desertdomes.com/tips.html

5. Assembling the Basic Dome

1. https://www.monolithic.org/products
2. http://www.stuartmcmillen.com/blog/chilling-domes-physics/

7. Adding Ferrocement

1. http://www.mortarsprayer.com/
2. http://www.mortarsprayer.com/spiderlath/
3. http://www.billboardtarps.com/

8. Extra Items

1. http://harmoniouspalette.com/BuildGreen.html

THE ULTIMATE GUIDE TO PEPPER SPRAY

How to Confidently Choose and Use the Best Less Lethal Defense

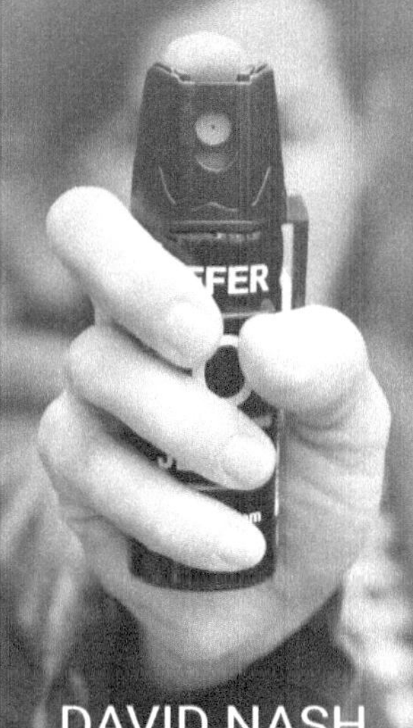

DAVID NASH

INTRODUCTION

If you asked me who I am, I would answer that I am a Dad. Being a family man is the most important aspect of my life. Providing for and protecting my family is what I see as my highest purpose. Luckily my career has allowed me to gather the skills and information to be able to effectively protect my family from the threats in life.

You see, I am a long time firearm instructor, a former US Marine, and a preparedness advocate. I have written several traditionally published books on firearm usage and disaster preparedness. This is my first self-published book, but I have taught this subject for nearly 20 years.

I own a private training school called the Shepherd School[1]. It originally began as a firearm school, but as my skills and certifications grew, so did my understanding of what it meant to protect my family. Guns are only one aspect of true preparedness and protection. I have to be able to bandage a wound, teach my child how to stay out of trouble, know how to put out a kitchen fire, get my family to shelter during a storm, and change a flat tire. Being the family protector is more than just being able to employ deadly force. I have that option if I need to use a gun, but what about those that can't carry a firearm, or don't want to?

My wife is a special education teacher. She couldn't carry a gun to work even if she wanted to. She doesn't want to. Unless someone was trying to hurt our son, I am not sure she could even draw a gun against another human. I wrote this as a guide for people like her. I want to give you some quality guidance on how to buy, carry, use, and decontaminate pepper spray. I make no judgments on your choices. I just want to help you feel (and be) safer.

I have been a pepper spray instructor for almost 17 years. My first experience with chemical agents was in 1993 when I entered the Gas Chamber at Paris Island. A year or so later I received my first dose of pepper spray while trying to impress a girl by showing off. She had a little can her daddy gave her when she went to college, and I wanted to show how it was not nearly as powerful as the stuff we used in the Marines. I was wrong on both accounts, she wasn't impressed and I learned the power of good pepper spray.

Later I became a correction officer, and then a chemical agent instructor. Over the years I have lost track of how many times I have been sprayed. I've been sprayed a lot, whether for training, or as a side effect of wrestling with someone being sprayed it hurts and is not fun. Currently I work as correction academy instructor, and we spray our cadets as a part of their formal pre-service training. With the understanding that comes from thousands of exposures to pepper spray as the person spraying, being sprayed, or helping decontaminate the sprayed individual both in and out of classroom settings, I can confidently say I have a good understanding of the mechanics of pepper spray usage. I also know what does doesn't help make it stop hurting.

I can also say I have heard almost every conceivable bad theory on pepper spray. This short book is designed to separate the rumors from the facts and to give the best advice possible.

1

WHAT IS PEPPER SPRAY?

Without going deep into the history of pepper's being used as a weapon, dried pepper powder was used by Japanese police in the mid 1800s to blind criminals.[1]

They used a small box with a mouthpiece to blow pepper powder at suspects. Our technology has greatly improved, and the formulas now contain the extracted chemical rather than just being a solution of ground pepper plant.

The active ingredient in pepper sprays is called oleoresin capsicum (OC) this chemical is extracted by using a solvent like ethanol and then the solvent is evaporated leaving the OC resin.

The resin is then suspended in a carrier liquid like water, oil, or alcohol and placed in the spray container. A propellant gas like butane is then used to pressurize the container so that the liquid can be expelled at an attacker.

Some formulas use flammable carriers or propellants that can be ignited if an electronic device like a stun-gun or TASER is used after OC spray exposure. Most OC manufacturers now use water instead of alcohol as a carrier liquid and inert gas such as nitrogen instead of butane as a propellant. However, many law enforcement agencies still test for flammability.

Oleoresin Capsicum is an Inflammatory Agent

OC is not Mace, Mace is a brand of chemical agent. The two less lethal chemical irritants (tear gas) in use are CS and CN.

OC is an inflammatory agent. It works differently.

CS Gas is actually a compound mainly used in military tear gas grenades. It is called 2-chlorobenzalmalononitrile.

CN is Phenacyl chloride and was invented in 1965 when a chemist's wife was threatened on the street. This turned into the Chemical Mace brand of self-defense sprays.[2]

It is important to know that CS and CN sprays are chemical irritants, they hurt, but it also takes some time for them to begin irritate the exposed person, so it takes a few seconds for them to begin to feel the pain. Chemical irritants are also is harder to decontaminate than OC.

OC is an inflammatory agent, it hurts of course, but its true purpose is to cause exposed mucus membranes to swell. This causes the eyes to swell shut so that an attacker cannot see. If the spray gets into the nose it makes it hard for the attacker to breathe.

If a person cannot see and is fighting to breathe, then their effectiveness in attacking the citizen is reduced considerably.

Add in the pain factor and many people panic when sprayed. An attacker in a mindless blind panic can be dangerous, but it also can allow you time to remove yourself from the situation.

Because OC is an inflammatory and not an irritant, it begins to work instantly when exposed to mucus membranes. As soon as it gets in the eyes the eyes swell shut and begin to hurt.

OC is also easier to clean off (decontaminate) than chemical agents. This is important in the even you get contaminated during a fight. For law enforcement agents it is vital because they arrested suspect can't be booked into jail until they are decontaminated and shorter clean up time means more time on patrol.

Some companies sell blends of OC and chemical agents, even including dyes for marking suspects. I have used OC/CS blends with some success, but I prefer stronger straight OC sprays. My preference is to have a spray that hits hard immediately, so I can get away or gain control, and then decontaminate rapidly so I don't have to suffer any longer than I have to (in a later section I will explain why I worded that as I did rather than say so the attacker won't suffer longer than necessary). Remember the justification in using OC spray is not to hurt people, but to render them less capable of hurting us.

Before we get into the strengths, types, and sizes of OC defensive spray options, I think it is vital to have the understanding of a good defensive mindset.

2

ARE YOU SURE YOU WANT TO CARRY PEPPER SPRAY

There are a few different reasons to carry Pepper Spray – You may carry pepper spray because you have a specific fear. That fear may be an angry ex-husband, protection while jogging, just in case... You may carry because you don't like guns, are afraid of guns, or you can't own a gun because of your age or other reasons. You may carry spray because it is not lethal and you are unwilling or unable to use deadly force. Some, like me, carry both a gun and a can of spray to have the flexibility of a two tiered response.

In the end it does not matter why you carry defensive sprays, as long as you understand the laws of using force and are willing to actually employ the tools you have. I work inside a prison as a trainer of new staff, so I am familiar with the common criminal mindsets. I know first-hand how effective felons are at reading weakness. If you choose to carry a defensive tool of any kind, you must first decide to use it if needed and to determine what actions would cause you to respond with force.

As my primary defensive tool is lethal, I have decided exactly what would cause me to potentially kill someone. I would not shoot a person over stuff. I would hand over my wallet to an armed robber in an instant, but I would kill or die before I would let them take my son as a hostage. A burglar can take my TV and leave, but if they approach the bedroom hallway I would respond with force.

I do the same type of contemplation with my spray, it is less than lethal, so the mental preparation is not as intense, but you should understand, that when you are involved in a fight you never know how it will turn out. For myself, I would never spray someone simply because I was mad at them, or they "creeped me out," but I would spray someone that grabbed me, tried to pull me into a dark alley, or tried to strike me. If you are in a threatening situation, you don't have time to think about cause and effect, you should already be familiar the law, understand justified self-defense, and know your capabilities.

If you are dependent on the tool to scare an attacker a way and don't have the fortitude to actually employee the device, an attacker will know that will respond accordingly. The answer to a criminal's question of "what you going to do with that," should be a strong, confident, and firm "Spray you if you don't stop!"

In short, don't carry it if you won't use it, and if you use it make sure you can explain why.

The legal standard for use of pepper spray is much lower than that of a gun, which makes it a valuable option. Most states do not regulate the ownership of pepper sprays, or have legal age limits for carrying. This is much different from handgun carry. Only one state in the US has no legal statute describing how to legally carry a handgun (Vermont).

In my state, for example, it is legal to use force to stop a theft or terminate a trespass, but you cannot use deadly force or even the threat of deadly force to do so. So, in Tennessee, if I caught someone stealing I could use OC spray to make them stop stealing. However, I would be committing a crime if I shot them, or even threatened to shoot them.

3

WHAT IS THE PROPER MINDSET?

Whole books could be, *and have been* written on the proper defensive mindset. Based on my experience and training, the right mindset is much more important that any tool you have at hand.

A proper mindset is noticed by attackers and often causes them to find an easier target.

First, and as we covered earlier, if you are going to carry a weapon, then you must be 100% willing to use it when needed.

Next you need to be smart. Know the law and understand what the reasonable man standard is.

If you have any defensive firearm training of any sort, you have to have heard the term "Reasonable Force" at some point. The reasonableness standard is probably the most important test when someone is trying to decide if your defensive action is justified or not.

However, you may ask just what is reasonable?

This is a large part of any self-defense training I provide because I believe it is a lot easier to teach an individual HOW to shoot than it is to teach the WHEN to shoot.

Each state has its own laws, and since I am a trainer and not an attorney so I cannot give you a legal opinion on the law, but based upon my training and experience as a firearm instructor I can give you some points of consideration for you to research on your own.

I also feel the need to inform you that my training is geared more toward armed professionals (Law Enforcement and Security), and that the majority of legal case law that I know is geared toward them. However, I do believe that many of the lessons learned from police shootings apply to civilians as long as the armed citizen understands the entire situation, including the legal differences between LE and citizen.

In my security classes I talk a lot about Tennessee vs. Garner[1] and Graham v. Conner[2], but they are just the starting point for learning about legal use of force.

We know that no single person is perfect, and as a group we are not perfect. There is no real person that we can hold to be perfectly reasonable 100% of the time, but by creating the legal fiction of a reasonable man. Our legal system can use this fiction as an objective tool to avoid subjective decisions. This creates a system where the law works in a foreseeable, uniform and neutral manner when attempting to determine fault.

The reasonable person standard assumes that each person has a duty to behave as any reasonable person would under the same or similar circumstances.

The law cannot predict specific circumstances of each case,

but the reasonable person standard does not change. You have act in a reasonable way, no matter what is happening.

The question that I s used to decide the reasonableness of an action is; would a reasonable (non-emotional) person, in the similar circumstances, with similar training act as you did.

This is not democratic, it is not about comparing your actions to that of the average person. The average person may be wrong (look at the last couple elections or the ratings for reality TV). The fictional Reasonable Person is not emotional nor subject to personal whim.

The Reasonable Person is Defined as:

The reasonable person is an ordinary, prudent person who normally exercises due care while avoiding extremes of both audacity and caution.

Used as a test of liability in cases of negligence, this standard is not applied uniformly on all persons because varying degrees of reasonableness may be expected from a minor (infant), an adult, an unskilled person, or a professional such as a doctor. See also prudent man rule.[3]

For citizens, it is important to know that you do not get to decide if your action is reasonable. Of course you think your action was right, otherwise you probably would not have done it.

The first person to decide on the reasonableness of your act will be the responding officer, then prosecutors, judges, the media, your family, friends, and the general public.

Considerations for the Reasonable Person:

- What is the foreseeable risk of harm his actions may create against the utility of his actions?
- What is the extent of the risk he is going to create?
- What is the likelihood such risk will actually cause harm to others?
- Are there any alternatives of lesser risk, and the costs of those alternatives?

Taking such actions requires the reasonable person to be informed, capable, aware of the law, and fair-minded. Such a person might do something extraordinary in certain circumstances, but whatever that person does or thinks it is always reasonable.

This is pretty hard for the average person to live up to without a certain amount of preplanning, training, and serious thought.

You are a reasonable person, so you have thought about your situation and made decisions you can explain. You know why you decided to carry OC spray instead of a gun, or OC Spray and a gun. You read the instructions on how to use it; you may have even practiced using your tool, or even taken a few classes.

Awareness is a Large Part of Proper Mindset

We aren't talking about guns specifically, but when I train people in firearms I point out that if you choose to carry a gun, every fight you get into is a gunfight because the person you are fighting may try to take your weapon?

This idea applies to anyone that decides to carry a defensive tool; even a less lethal one like OC spray or a TASER, you must stay aware of your situation and what is around you.

In my book **Handguns for Self-defense**, I spend a lot of time discussing mindset and awareness and because it applies to all manner of defensive tools and actions I will cover it here.

Two basic mental tools can help a person understand situational awareness. While they both describe the same idea the same way, you rarely hear of them at the same time.

These tools are the color code system popularized by the late gun-training icon Colonel Jeff Cooper and the National Rifle Association awareness levels as taught in their Personal Protection in the Home curriculum. For purposes of clarity, I have included them both in the following chart.

As you move up the levels of the chart, certain changes take place. This happens because the more your mind becomes ready to fight, the more it prepares your body to fight.

At this time, all you need to know is that the higher you move up the levels of alertness, the less you are able to perform complex tasks or critical thinking. If you have ever been unexpectedly scared and get jolted to the point where you are not sure what to do then you have experienced the flight/flight/flee response. The more levels you jump at a time, the slower you are to respond and the greater impact will be to your body.

It is easier to get ready to fight if you are expecting a threat. It is harder to make good tactical decisions when you are surprised and have to jump from being unaware of a threat to being ambushed by it.

Condition White/Unaware

In condition white you are going with the flow, unaware of anything outside your immediate human impulses. Basically you are unaware of what's going on around you. You are not ready. This condition, sadly, is the one most citizens live in for their entire lives. There are some situations where this is unavoidable. Sleeping, for example, is an activity where it is impossible for you to be in a higher level of awareness. While there is no moral connotation of evil attached to this level of awareness, it is not the proper mindset of a person concerned with his or her own safety. Anytime you are outside your home you should strive to not be unaware. This is especially true if you feel the need to carry a defensive tool like OC Spray. How can you justify carrying a weapon and not staying aware of threats?

Condition Yellow/Aware

If you are in condition yellow, you are alert, but are also calm and relaxed. In this level of awareness, you are scanning your surroundings for threats. You know who's in front of you, to your sides, and behind you.

It is important to understand that at the awareness level you are not anticipating an attack, but you are mentally ready in case of one. With practice, you can maintain this level of awareness for extended periods of time.

This is the best compromise between readiness and exertion. Higher levels of preparedness are meant for actual threats and not for long term.

Condition Orange/Alert

If you go to condition Orange, then you have a specific sense of unease. Something is not right. Something has alerted you to danger. Perhaps there are a number of suspicious men standing around your car. Or in the classic Jeff Cooper example, a guy wearing a raincoat comes into your shop on a sweltering summer day. What's wrong with this picture?

In the Orange level, you are aware of the positions of all potentially hostile people around you, as well as any weapons they may be able to use, either in their hands or within their reach. You are developing a plan for dealing with the potential hostilities: "...first I spray the guy walking toward me, and then I run north away from his friends standing around the park..." You may have also identified escape routes, depending on what response you will use. In addition to being mentally ready, you are physically ready as well.

In the NRA system at this level, you have pre-decided "trigger-points" that cause you to move to the next higher level of awareness. I whole-heartedly endorse this type of thinking. At this level of stress, it is hard to make complex decisions, especially when your decision involves life and death consequences with their respondent legal ramifications.

Condition Red/Alarm

If you are sitting at the Alarm phase then the fight is on. You are being actively attacked. There is little time for thinking or second-guessing your decisions.

Do what you need to do to survive.

There are only three ways to prepare for this: practice, practice, and practice. Bruce Lee once said,"I fear not the man who has practiced 10,000 kicks once, but I fear the man who has practiced one kick 10,000 times." You have to burn your actions into your muscles so that when the time comes you don't have to think about how to run your gun.

Remember when you first started driving. It took thought to

start the car, to put it in gear, to navigate through town. What would have happened if a dog ran out in front of you your first week of driving? After 10 years or so of driving every day, has it changed? Do you have to think about starting your car or do you just get in and drive?

If you're going to fight, you do not have time to figure out how to draw or what your sight picture should look like, you need to be in the fight.

Time Critical Decisions

Once you understand the importance of defensive awareness you should start to learn how to make decisions under stress. One well-used tool comes from the military and is called the OODA Loop.

In the 1950's a young USAF fighter pilot named John Boyd, who was cocky even by fighter-pilot standards, issued a standing challenge to all comers: starting from a position of disadvantage, he'd have his jet on their tail within 40 seconds, or he'd pay out $40. Legend has it that he never lost. His unfailing ability to win any dogfight in 40 seconds or less earned him his nickname, "40 Second" Boyd.

While undoubtedly this Air Force pilot had a high level of skill with his fighting tool, what made him great was that he knew how to make decisions quickly and accurately under stress.

The Air Force was so impressed with his skills they had him create a formal briefing to share this knowledge with the other pilots. This short briefing turned into a larger course taught at the Air Force Academy.

His system has been partially credited for the outstanding

success of the American fighter pilots in the Korean War. Colonel Boyd's system is called the OODA Loop. OODA is simply an acronym for Observe, Orientate, Decide, and Act.

- *Observe* - A creepy guy is always in the park where you take your daily run.(Yellow).
- *Orientate* - Is he approaching you? Is he a threat? (Upgrade to Orange), or is he homeless or waiting for someone (stay at Yellow)?
- *Decide* - Does the situation call for force, retreat, or no action? What are you going to do in the situation? How are you going to do this? If you followed my earlier advice and created pre-designated actions based upon certain "trigger-points" your response would be made even faster.
- *Act* - Do it! Act decisively and with purpose. I have seen a lot of people hurt because they took "Half-steps" because they were afraid of getting into trouble.

The OODA Loop explains the mechanism of decision-making. The basis of how it applies to self-defense is simple. Once you understand how your attacker makes decisions, you can get inside his OODA and do things that force him to reorient himself so that you can gain a speed advantage.

Basically, you want to make your attacker react to you rather than play catch-up to him. Instead of allowing your attacker to act, change the environment to force him to reorient himself. If you are able to do this, it will seem like your attacker is moving in slow motion because you will begin to act while he is reacting to you. This can be easier said than done, but it is an area that deserves attention.

If someone thinks of you as a harmless object to control, and you respond with confidence and force (and the appropriate tools) then you effectively "get inside their OODA" it will force them to reconsider their approach….

It takes longer to react than to act

The main purpose of all this awareness and decision making talk is to help you create a reactionary gap. No matter what level of awareness you start at, when attacked you are going to jump automatically to Alarm/Red. Imagine being awakened to a man on top of you with a knife to your throat.

This is a classic example of a condition White to Red response. Being more aware allows you to RECOGNIZE a threat while there is still time to take appropriate action (note, this is not always force; sometimes the appropriate action is leaving the scene, or even submitting). Whatever you action you choose, you will need time to implement it.

If you have created those mental trigger points, have confidence in your skills, awareness of your surroundings and situation; you are way ahead of the game. So much so that in all likelihood any potential criminal can tell you're not an easy target and will not put you in the situation to start with.

Could I Spray Someone?

Being prepared to act violently is not the same as wanting to act violently. One of my favorite quotes is from John Wayne in the movie *The Shootist*, "I won't be wronged, I won't be insulted, and I won't be laid a hand on. I don't do these things to other people, and I require the same from them."

90% of us live by some version of the Golden Rule, and are good guys at some base level. Don't forget that some people in society are bad people that like to do bad things. We need to cultivate a defensive mindset. Responsible people should determine in advance the level of force they are willing to use against someone who is attempting to harm our family or ourselves. Being ready to protect a loved one is not the same as wanting, desiring, or planning to kill.

I will not train someone who wants to hurt innocent people. I can't teach someone that doesn't understand the difference between justified and unjustified force and is not willing to learn. I preach avoidance, preparedness, deterrence, and that force is a last resort. I also believe that if it gets to the point where force is necessary, you must use enough of it to end the incident. Failure to follow through and end the attack will only cause more suffering and pain.

Andy vs. Barney

My mother once said that a lot of today's problems could be solved if school kids watched 30 minutes of the Andy Griffith show each day. I think she's right; there is a lot of good tactical knowledge to be gained from this old show. I use the Barney/Andy analogy quite often in my law enforcement classes.

It seems like in almost every episode of the Andy Griffith show a bad guy laughed at Barney, or Barney negligently fired into the ground trying to quick draw his pistol? On the other hand, Sheriff Taylor stopped almost every crime without using his gun?

That's TV, and isn't 100 accurate to real life, but the difference of mindset and the reaction people gave the two is realistic. That difference is based upon confidence. Andy did not need to prove how tough he is, he knew exactly what he can do, so he does not need to prove it at every chance. Barney feels like he gets his authority from his weapon, so he uses it like a crutch.

A can of pepper spray is just a high-powered hot sauce. It's your mindset that makes the difference. You build that mindset by training and deep contemplation on what you would or wouldn't do to protect you own or your loved one's life.

4

COPS ARE SPRAYED DURING TRAINING, DO I NEED TO BE?

Whenever I am either taking or teaching a pepper spray class I always hear at least 10% of the class comment that the reason they have to get sprayed is so that everyone knows how it feels like so that no one abuses the spray. That might not be the exact words used, but the idea that security or law enforcement has to feel the pain caused by pepper spray so they don't become abusive annoys me.

First off, if this is true, why stop with spray. Let's shoot all the police when they are in training… I mean, if a police recruit learns firsthand what a .40 to the chest feels like, they won't be tempted to shoot the wrong person… (The argument doesn't make sense in this light does it)

Secondly, if a police administrator has to use pain to create empathy and prevent abuse then they hired the wrong cadet or retained the wrong cop. They need some serious revisions to their human resource policies and training standards.

There are two reasons someone that carries less lethal sprays or TASERS need to experience them in training (and one is a minor reason).

Law Enforcement/Security personnel may need to be able to testify that they have an intimate understanding of the effects, and by being able to say they have been subject to the effects themselves, they can show that while painful, less lethal options are much more preferable to baton strikes or bullet hits. Personally I don't worry about that – I am not an administrator and don't concern myself with what some government lawyer would say about my actions.

Frankly I would not use force unless it is needed, and am not the type to use more physical force than I felt was needed to control a situation.

The true reason I want my students to get sprayed in training is for their own protection. I have NEVER been in a fight involving spray that either I, or someone on my team did not get exposed. Sprays tend to cross contaminate anyone near the fight. If you have never been sprayed, you will not know how to react to being sprayed. In my first OC spray instructor certification, not only did we get sprayed, we had to find the door back to get back inside the classroom, find a box near that door, dig through it to find a handcuff key, confront and control a hostile subject, subdue and handcuff them, double lock and then unlock the cuffs, and then find our way to the restroom where we could finally decontaminate ourselves. That was not fun, and it was not easy.

After that, I know that if I have to fight someone after being sprayed, I will be able to. I know I can take someone down and handcuff them, even if I myself am half blind from OC spray.

This matters because I also know that spray is not some wonder tool that ensures compliance, I know how effective TASERS are, but also how fast I can recover from one after being hit. Because I have been tased 4 times, I know exactly what they do. I know that they require a solid hit to work. In short, by experiencing the force option personally, I grow my own confidence in my ability to work while gaining personal knowledge of the weakness of the particular system.

In the end, I guess the "we are getting sprayed so we know what it is like" is true on some level. Unfortunately the words may be the same, but the difference in perspective is gravely different and engender two different mindsets and end results.

5

WHAT TYPE OF SPRAY SHOULD I BUY?

Short answer, it depends. There are different strengths, formulations, sizes, and probably the most important spray patterns and types to consider. Each type has its own strengths and weaknesses so let's take a few moments to talk about Strengths and Spray patterns.

How is OC Spray Strength Measured?

There are currently three ways manufacturers promote the strength/concentration of their particular brand of OC spray.

- Percentage of OC
- Scoville Heat Units (SHU's)
- Capsaicinoid Concentration

These three methods are listed from least accurate to most accurate. Most all law enforcement agencies in the US only use Capsaicinoid Concentration as a method of determining how "strong" a spray is.

.   .   .

THE PERCENTAGE METHOD measures the amount OC by volume in a given solution.

The Pungency (heat) varies from due to pepper type and quality.

Because of this it is possible for a lower concentration of OC in a solution to feel "hotter" than a higher OC concentration solution. OC percentage is not a reliable indicator of product strength.

In common terms, which is hotter to your tongue, a chili made with 50% beans and 50% sweet bell pepper or a chili made with 90% beans and 10% ghost pepper?

Lower quality manufactures can use the percentage measurement to mislead consumers.

Scoville Heat Units (SHU's) is a measurement of perceived heat when a pepper product is placed on the tongue. This measurement is based on a scoring system assigned by a panel of five tasters from the American Spice Trade Association. As a reference here are some common peppers and their SHU rating:

- Green bell peppers 0 SHU's
- Jalapeno 5,000 SHU's
- Tabasco 30,000-50,000 SHU's
- Habanero 250,000-350,000 SHU's
- Bhut Jolokia (Ghost Pepper) 1,041,427 SHU
- Carolina Reaper 2,200,000 SHU

Unfortunately, Since SHU rating is based on the perception of heat rather than an exact measurement, the rating could vary from one panel to another. I used to sell Fox Lab's OC spray in the early/mid 2000s and their claim to fame was their 5.3 million SHU rating. I have been sprayed by Fox Lab's sprays several times and let me tell you they are HOT. I was a strong believer in SHU rating until I learned about the more scientific Capsaicinoid Concentration measurement.

CAPSAICINOID CONCENTRATION MEASURES the amount of the actual capsaicinoids in a product. This is the unit of measurement that is the most consistent and best representation throughout all grades of Oleoresin Capsicum.[1]

Major capsaicinoids can only be guaranteed through High Performance Liquid Chromatography (HPLC) testing.

When I left Emergency Management and went back to the Correction field I had to attend the basic correctional officer academy. It was there that I was introduced to the concept of measuring the concentration, and that the hottest available spray in our Department was called Sabre Red[2]. I asked how the 1.33 percent Sabre Red compared to the 5.3 Million SHU Fox Lab rating. Without missing a beat, the drill instructor said, "It is comparable".

As the group leader of my class, when it was time to get sprayed, I went first and when asked "regular or extra-crispy" I volunteered to take the 1.33 Sabre Red instead of the lesser formula.

As soon as the spray hit my eyes I raised my hand and said,"I have made a mistake, don't take the extra-crispy" the young guys in the class laughed and thought I was joking.

I was not.

Upon promotion to becoming an Academy Instructor I had a

discussion with that particular Instructor and related that while it is technically true that a Geo Metro has 4 wheels just like a Ferrari, it is unfair to say they are comparable when asked which would be a good first car.

OC Spray Patterns

There are different delivery systems that have spray patterns that have specific strengths and weaknesses in areas such as distance, accuracy, wind resistance, and blowback.

OC Pepper spray manufactures typical produce two basic spray patterns and two additional delivery systems besides a water based spray.

They are:

- Stream
- Cone Mist
- Foam
- Gel

THE STREAM PATTERN has the best range, generally 12-15 feet. It looks like the solid stream from a water gun, so breezes and winds do not easily affect it. This means is it less likely to blow back in your face. The single stream makes it easier to aim, but aiming is more necessary.

The recommended spray method for a stream of OC is to arc across the eyebrows (ear to ear) with the spray covering the eyes as a primary target.

One thing to be aware of with a ballistic stream is the hydraulic needle effect. It is strongly recommended that any aerosol discharged towards the facial area be limited to a safe distance of 3 feet because the stream may have enough force to inject itself into the first layers of the eye leading to permanent injury. However, if someone is trying to kill you, and OC spray is all you have, then you may have no choice but to spray at the dangerous distance. If lethal force was justifiable in a situation, and this was all you had, then blinding an attacker could be legally justified.

THE CONE **mist pattern** is easier to aim, because it has a wider spray pattern and finer droplets than stream. It comes out in a tight group, but spreads wider as the distance from the can increases. Because of the fine droplets it only has a range of 8 to 10 feet.

This cone of mist creates a pepper spray barrier that can impact multiple attackers, but a mild breeze can affect your ability to hit your target, and may come back on the sprayer.

The recommended spray method for a cone mist is to spray with a controlled motion from nose to mouth. Once you spray to hit your target, move away.

Cone mist is best used indoors because of its weakness in the wind.

THE FOAM DELIVERY **system** has an effective range of 8-10 feet. It comes out like shaving cream. This is used because it has a much smaller chance of being inhaled and is easier to clean up areas after spraying someone.

The problem is that foam can be scooped up by the target and thrown back at the sprayer. It is also very slippery on waxed or linoleum floors.

OC Gel was designed to enhance OC foam; it is sticky and coats the target when applied. It has the longest range of any spray, 15-20 feet and the weight of the gel makes it wind resistant.

However, unlike foam that will drip down behind an attacker's glasses, gel sticks and will stay where it is applied.

Primary target is the eye; concentrate aim between the eyes to be sure both are covered

6

WHAT ARE THE LAWS ON PEPPER SPRAY?

I am not a lawyer, and laws change over time, but I wanted to give a brief overview of the specific state laws concerning OC sprays at the time of publishing. Please take a moment to review the specific laws of your state before you carry OC spray.

It is a federal offense to carry/ship pepper sprays on a commercial airliner or to carry it beyond the security checkpoint at the airport.

Pepper spray may only be used in situations involving imminent physical threats or fear of bodily harm and may not be used to prevent theft or in situations of verbal abuse.

US Pepper Spray Laws

Pepper spray can be legally purchased and carried in all 50 states. Some states do regulate the maximum allowed strength of the pepper spray, age restriction, content and usage.

Alaska:[1]

Cannot be carried in a school unless over 21 years old.

. . .

ARKANSAS:[2]

Pepper spray container must be less than 5 oz.

California:[3]

California Penal Code, Section 12403.7, as of January 1, 1996, and as a result of Assembly Bill 830 (Speier), the pepper spray and mace programs are now deregulated.

California Penal Code Section 12400 - 12460 govern pepper spray use in California. Container holding the defense spray must contain no more than 2.5 ounces (71 g) net weight of aerosol spray.

Pepper spray may only be used in situations involving imminent physical threats or fear of bodily harm and may NOT be used to prevent theft or in situations of verbal abuse.

Certain individuals are still prohibited from possessing pepper spray, including minors under the age of 16, convicted felons, individuals convicted of narcotic/drug addiction, individuals convicted of assault, and individuals convicted of misusing pepper spray.

A police officer may cite or arrest a person who does not comply with regulations stated on the pepper or mace product.

Florida: [4]

Any pepper spray containing no more than 2 ounces of chemical can be carried in public openly or concealed without a permit. Furthermore, any such pepper spray is classified as "self-defense chemical spray" and therefore not considered a weapon under Florida law.

Hawaii:[5]

Pepper spray container cannot be larger than 1/2 oz. License required.

Michigan:[6]

Michigan allows "reasonable use" of spray containing not more than 10% oleoresin capsicum to protect "a person or property under circumstances that would justify the person's use of physical force".

It is illegal to give a "self-defense spray" to a person under 18 years of age.

Nevada:[7]

2 oz. container limit on CS tear gas, pepper spray is exempt.

NEW YORK:[8]

OC can be legally possessed by any person age 18 or over. No more than 0.67% capsaicin content allowed

It must be purchased in person (i.e., cannot be purchased by mail-order or internet sale) either at a pharmacy or from a licensed firearm retailer and the seller must keep a record of purchases.

The use of pepper spray to prevent a public official from performing his/her official duties is a class-E felony.

New Jersey:[9]

Non-felons over the age of 18 can possess a small amount of

pepper spray, with no more than three-quarters of an ounce of chemical substance.

North Carolina:

When carrying for protection against people, container cannot be larger than 5 ounces.

Washington: [10]

Persons over 18 may carry personal-protection spray devices.

Persons over age 14 may carry personal-protection spray devices with their legal guardian's consent.

Wisconsin: [11]

Tear gas is not permissible.

By regulation, OC products with a maximum OC concentration of 10% and weight range of oleoresin of capsicum and inert ingredients of 15-60 grams are authorized.

This is 1/2 and 2 oz. (14 and 57 g) spray. Further, the product cannot be camouflaged, and must have a safety feature designed to prevent accidental discharge. The units may not have an effective range of over 20 feet and must have an effective range of six feet.

In addition there are certain labeling and packaging requirements, it must state cannot sell to anyone under 18 and the phone number of the manufacturer has to be on the label. The units must also be sold in sealed tamper-proof packages.

7

WHY NOT JUST BUY WASP SPRAY?

I don't care what the news reporters, your aunt Mabel, or the guy down the street that used to be a cop tells you. Using wasp spray as a "cheap" pepper spray alternative is a terrible idea.

The self-defense training world has a lot of people that speak without understanding. I can't count the times I have heard things such as,"my buddy the cop said I should…" It is doubtful your cop buddy would testify in open court that he told you do something ignorant or illegal.

Some instructors or online content creators don't care about the quality of information and teach questionable material to make a few bucks on tuition.

On the subject of bad ideas, I read a lot of internet bloggers mention using wasp spray as a cheap alternative to OC spray. Using wasp spray against a human is using a chemical outside of its designed use and as such is against federal regulation. It is not a reasonable act, and you may be held liable for any injury from using something not safe for humans on humans.

Wasp spray is designed to KILL, it shares many characteristics and precursor chemicals with chemical weapons used for mass destruction. OC spray is designed to be less than lethal and is held to be safe for use on people.

Now, realistically, if the deranged crack-head felon that lives near my land comes and attacks me while I am out working at the land and I have a can of wasp spray because I was cleaning out wasp nests, then I may use it as a weapon of opportunity. But that is much different from choosing to save a couple dollars by choosing to carry and use a poison instead of a tested product.

To illustrate the concept a little further, in my state it is clearly against the law to carry a club or baton for the purpose of self-defense. I don't recommend it, and I don't recommend carrying a bat in the car "just in case". However, I have a son in T-ball, and he has a bat, a glove, and a ball. We keep it in the car because otherwise they don't make it to practice. This isn't a "wink-wink" I found a way to bend a law, but an actual reality of my life. If I needed to use a bat to protect my family, I am confident in my ability to explain why the bat was there to a jury.

The wasp spray is an illegal substitute for OC spray, just as it is illegal to carry a bat for self-defense in Tennessee. I may be able to get away with either if the situation is such that it is all I have and I am justified in severely injuring or killing my attacker. However, a prosecutor and most likely a jury will look VERY closely at the circumstances. If I used wasp spray to save a few bucks then I will most likely pay severely for that savings.

8

HOW SHOULD I CARRY PEPPER SPRAY?

You should carry your spray in a way that is easy to access while being out of sight.

This means you should not stick a can in your pants pocket, you won't be able to get to it in a rapidly evolving attack.

I personally don't like sticking a small can on my keys.

Keeping it on my keys does ensure I always have it near by, but it's awkward to get the can orientated so I can spray it. I know some people really like it. If the convenience is important to you then I suggest you get a break away key chain. Also be careful to buy a can with a safety cap. If you ever accidentally spray yourself you won't question why.

If you carry OC spray while jogging, a great carry solution is a wrist holster.

They make several types, some are more stylish that the one pictured.

I have even seen a bracelet that contained a small OC canister inside the band. After researching it I decided it was a novelty, but the point is there are a lot of hands free devices designed to be worn while exercising.

The way I prefer to carry my pepper spray is in a holster on the belt. That's probably because of my corrections background, but its easy to get to, and I hind that in todays world of people living in condition white with cell phones strapped on like batman's utility belt, its rather inconspicuous as long as you are not constantly touching and fiddling with the holster. I have seen a lot of people talk about carrying the holster and spray upside down to make drawing faster. I can't fault the idea for speed. It is faster. However, as a bigger guy, gravity is not my friend. I carry mine right side up so it can't possibly fall out of the holster.

Most people I know that carry pepper spray simply put it in their purse. I know that's how my wife carries. That's probably the best compromise option. A woman almost always has her purse, the spray is concealed, and if some thought is put into where it is placed and not just dropped in the bag a can is easy to access. I, and many other instructors' recommend clipping it to an inside front pocket. That way it is at the top for easy and quick usage. Additionally, if you have long purse straps, you can place your hand inside the purse and hold on to the can with the purse still on your shoulder. That's great for those code orange times when you get a "creeper" vibe or just have a gut feeling that something is off.

No matter how you decide to carry the spray, make sure you practice drawing the can and presenting it to a target. What works well in theory tends to fail in the intensity of an actually attack if it has never actually had the kinks worked out of the system.

Also in with the carrying, this isn't something to get and forget. Cans expire, and they leak.

There should be an expiration date on the bottom of the can, If an expiration date is not presence I write a date 3 years past when I purchased it. I also look at the nozzle for signs of leakage.

In the department I currently work for we also weigh the cans upon issuance, at turn in, and after use. Few things are worse than needing your pepper spray and it dribbles out because it is almost empty.

9

HOW DO I USE MY SPRAY?

R emember, that pepper spray is a defensive tool. It is considered a less lethal weapon, but it is nevertheless a weapon. It should never be used as a punishment of for harassment. A person can make you mad, but spraying them just because of that will likely end in a charge of assault against you.

Now that the mandatory legal disclaimer is out of the way, if you do feel threatened start by first gripping the canister.

The best way is to wrap your hand around the can and using the thumb on the spray actuator.

This may feel awkward, but it allows you to reposition the thumb and use your fist should you have to use hand-to-hand defensive techniques.

It is also much more secure. Using your index finger on top to make the can spray feels more natural but it is much easier for an aggressor to rip the spray can out of your hand.

I know that sounds crazy, you may be thinking, "How can a

person fight after being sprayed?" Believe me they can, I have the bruises to prove it. Never trust any tool 100% and always have a back up plan.

I have been sprayed many times, and as an instructor I typically have to perform self-defense maneuvers after being sprayed.

It hurts, and I am functionally blind, but if an old, out of shape, fat guy can fight after being sprayed, you must bet that a young motivated attacker can also.

Steps for Using Spray:

Give a verbal warning, it can give you confidence, cause an attacker to find easier prey, and it helps the reasonability argument.

A strong and forceful back off or I WILL spray you is what you're looking for.

Next aim for the face, the eyes specifically. If the attacker is taller and you can angle up into the nose the impact will be highly magnified. A slash across both eyes is enough, however, I know a particularly tough Academy Drill Instructor that does a "Z" pattern. They spray of across the eyes, down the nose, and across the mouth. That works well, but the more you spray the higher chances you will get exposed through cross contamination.

Your first action after spraying your attacker is to break off and add distance. Hopefully, you can gain enough distance that you end up at the local police department and he ends up in jail. However, sometimes things go wrong and the attacker is able to get close.

If that happens do not be afraid to strike your attacker with the can if the spray itself did not work.

In the pepper spray uses I have been involved in most times that that spray did not get the desired effect the officer involved shook the can up and re-sprayed the subject, they did so over and over. Spray, Shake, Spray, Shake, Spray, Shake, Ad nauseam.

If the spray did not work the first time, you may have not gotten it in the eyes. If the situation warrants, try again. However if a second spray doesn't work then a third fourth or fifth attempt is also unlikely to work.

I have dealt with inmates that after being sprayed, wiped their eyes with their hand, licked their fingers and said, "Ummm good". If that is the case, then go to plan "B". Specifically if your attacker does this I would suggest start moving rapidly in the opposite direction, or alternatively if you can't run away Bop them in the face with the bottom of the can….

Essentials of Using Pepper Spray:

- Always aim for the eyes and face.
- Be sure to spray the eyes, but more might not be better.
- A spray can take a second to take effect. The effect is instantaneous once it gets in the eyes, but if they were closed it may take a second to get in them.
- Spray from a distance and then move as far and as fast as possible.
- Never rub your own eyes.
- Pepper spray does expire.

10

HOW DO I DECONTAMINATE OTHERS OR MYSELF?

When my cadets learn they have to be "exposed" to OC spray they are universally worried about getting sprayed. I don't blame them pepper spray hurts. In all honestly I would always choose a TASER over pepper spray (and I've been tased more than a few times myself). However, from personal experience I have tried just about every method for taking the burn away. I have sold commercial decontamination wipes and sprays. I have poured milk all over my head. I have followed the procedures in a scientific paper published by the Poison Control Center using Milk of Magnesia, as well as all manner of soaps and shampoos.

In all seriousness, I can unequivocally state that nothing makes it hurt less.

As I will explain a little later, time is the best and most reliable way of relieving the pain of exposure to Oleoresin Capsicum.

Even with the most potent law enforcement 1.33% sprays

after about 40 minutes I will regain full function. However, with the procedure outlined below, I can cut that down to about 10 minutes. 10 minutes of burning eyes is still a long time. To compare, while the pain is (at least to me) slightly less than the 50,000-volt electrical jolt of a TASER, a Law Enforcement TASER ride is only 5 seconds.

Why Do I Have to Know How to Decontaminate OC?

In a perfect world you won't, but we don't live in a perfect world. You could accidentally activate your can while digging for it in your purse, your child could accidentally discover it. If you are like my poor long-suffering wife your husband may accidentally activate it while checking it for leaks…

A more likely scenario is that the wind blows some into your face as you actually use it, or a spray soaked bad guys spits and snots OC residue and you get it on you as you fight.

It really doesn't really matter HOW you got exposed. If you ever get OC in your face, your concern will be how to get it OFF.

Decontamination Protocol

If you have every misjudged just how hot your Nashville hot chicken actually was you know how soothing a big cold class of water is. Until you drink all the water and the burn intensifies.

What you need to know is that Oleoresin Capsicum is the *oily resin* of hot pepper.

Water doesn't do anything for OC spray either.

The idea that milk is a base and will soothe an acid burn is a good idea, except OC spray doesn't hurt because it is an acid so Milk does nothing either.

You need to get the oil off the body.

Dawn dishwashing soap is the most effective thing I have found to wash the oil off, but it is a little harsh on my eyes. Baby shampoo is what my experience finds to be the best option. It cuts oil well, and is gentle enough to pour directly on the eye, which is something I have seen people do.

Get some soap on your hands and lather it on the eyebrows, eyes, and the immediately adjoining facial areas. There is no sense in trying to wash the entire face. It is more likely that not that you will just spread the OC to you lips and mouth then get it all off.

Rinse the soap off.

Next, get out of the water. Seriously, get out of the water. I know you will not want to, I never want to either. While the cool water splashes your face you will think its helping. It isn't it is like that water at the restaurant. It is tricking you. True relief comes with time. As long as you are in the water you are not allowing the OC spray to deactivate.

Some rub the water off their face, those people tend to look red and puffy the next day as towels and rough scrubbing irritate the eyes. Personally I drip dry. It is easier, and at this point I am really not caring about how I look.

After you get out of the water the best thing you can do is take your fingers and pry your eyes open. You may think your eyes are swollen shut and it is not possible to open them. You would be half right. Once you get them open the first time, they will immediately shut. It will be easier to open the next time. Keep prying them open until you can open your eyes without your fingers prying them open. Once you can open them, regardless of how long you can keep the open, start blinking.

At this point blinking will be difficulty, but it will become easier.

Your goal is to rapidly "strobe" your eyes until they tear up. Tears are your goal. Blinking rapidly will cause tears to form.

Tears contain an enzyme that helps clear the eyes. This will work wonders for removing the last traces of the oleoresin.

You will be surprised how quickly rapid blinking will relieve your eye discomfort.

During all of this many people panic. If your attacker panics when he gets a face-full of spray then maybe you will help persuade him to find a new line of work. However, panic is makes the pain seem worse. Panic robs you of confidence and the ability to make good decisions.

Panic is the worse thing you can allow at this point. Luckily there are breathing exercises that both help keep you calm AND reduce the chances you inhale any pepper spray residue.

I find that with the soaping and blinking procedure above, the following breathing technique really helps with successfully dealing with an OC exposure.

This is called combat breathing, and while it is commonly taught in advanced self-defense courses, I first learned of it in Col Dave Grossman's book **On Combat**.[1]

The idea is to breathe in a cycle of 4, 4-second deep breaths in through the mouth, hold, and then breathe out through the nose for a 4 count. Repeat.

After a few cycles the deep oxygen exchange will tend to clear your head and calm you down. I know I do it when the boy acts up and I need to take a second.

An additional benefit from breathing out from the nose tends to keep you from inhaling any pepper spray residue.

It is of great importance not to get the two confused.

Last time I got sprayed I volunteered to go first and since my blinking got me workable pretty fast I went around helping my fellow students. I was loudly extolling the virtues of breathing and staying calm. "in through your mouth, out through your nose…." At some point I got twisted up and reversed the procedure. Well, I paid for my confusion as I sucked up a big blob of water/OC mix.

The pain of pepper to the eyes is nothing on what it is in the lungs. I almost gagged hard enough to vomit out my own toes…

In my defense, I failed the system; the system did not fail me.

Almost monthly I have former students tell me that the OC decontamination system "really works". They generally add that they thought I was just talking in class, and/or they took a while to try it in real life. Keep it in the back of your head, because if you ever get sprayed you will want to stay calm and get it off of you as soon as you can.

11

HOW TO DECONTAMINATE ITEMS

The following works, and works well. However, it is not for your personal decontamination of OC spray. It is NOT safe for use on your face or any sensitive areas.

In making **hot sauces** and other things that use hot peppers I am getting used to accidentally contaminating sensitive areas of my body with oleoresin capsicum.

If you have ever watched any of my **YouTube videos** on making hot sauce you might have heard me warning my help not to rub their eyes after using hot peppers. Without fail they always seem to get burned. It almost always happens after they wash their hands and think they have the hot pepper resin off of their hands. Usually the burning happens when they go to the bathroom.

I got tired of feeling guilty for laughing at my young non-listening nephew or getting in trouble by my pretty but non-listening wife. I decided to do some research to see how to cook with peppers without getting burned and the solution is actually pretty simple.

Hand Soap doesn't do much to remove the oleoresin capsicum from skin, generally only time works. Fortunately since it is an OILY resin it is possible to saponify it (turn the resin into soap).

Much like using sodium hydroxide to turn fat to soap calcium hydroxide (in bleach) can make the oil water-soluble.

If you mix a 10% beach solution using bleach and water and dip your hands in the solution from time to time as you are working with peppers it will make the resin into something close to soap. It will feel slippery but will rinse clean with water.

Once again, do NOT use the bleach on sensitive areas like your eyes or genitalia, and make sure you wash the bleach off very thoroughly.

Use common sense and I think you will be very pleased. The first time I tried this **I made a video of the process** and was very surprised it actually worked since nothing else seems to.

I tried this (well a version of this using a less caustic chemical) to get the same saponification process last time I got pepper sprayed for certification. The science was valid, it was well documented in a paper from the poison control center (using milk of magnesia), unfortunately it did not work.

I do know, from experience, and from the video above, that bleach solution DOES work on the hands and kitchen utensils to allow you to cook with peppers without getting burned.

It clearly removes the hot pepper oil off of surfaces. Once again for the record, DO NOT use it around the eyes or mucus membranes this method is for things not beings.

AFTERWORD

I hope this book was useful to you. I wanted a book that covered the basics, was easily understood, was not dull, and had very little fluff.

My wife says I am not a funny as I think I am, so some of my anecdotes may have not been as entertaining as I hoped, but regardless the information comes from years of experience.

How many people will let their **wife pepper spray them** so they can tape giving a basic pepper spray class while experiencing the burn of OC to the eyes? If this eBook wasn't enough information you can see me doing just that.

If you got anything out of this book I hope it was how important proper defensive mindset is to surviving attacks, that OC spray is a good tool when lethal force is not available or legally justified, that you need to practice carrying and using your spray, and that you can get exposed and not panic.

It should go without saying, but I will say it just to be clear. The information presented in this book comes from years of experience and formal training, but the opinions expressed are mine alone and do not represent any individual department or agency.

NOTES

1. Introduction

1. https://shepherdpublish.com/self-published-works/21-days-to-basic-preparedness/

2. Personal Preparedness Mindset

1. https://www.tngun.com/completed-incremental-disaster-kit/

3. Types of Emergency Kits

1. https://www.tngun.com/prn-40-alphabet-kits/

6. Must Have Essentials for a Get Home Bag

1. https://en.wikipedia.org/wiki/Mors_Kochanski
2. https://www.tngun.com/list-of-edc-lists/
3. https://www.tngun.com/essential-gear-for-a-get-home-bag/

Introduction

1. **https://www.tngun.com**

1. What is Pepper Spray?

1. **http://www.historyofwar.org/articles/weapons_metsubishi.html**
2. **https://www.smithsonianmag.com/history/forgotten-history-mace-designed-29-year-old-and-reinvented-police-weapon-180953239/**

3. What is the Proper Mindset?

1. https://en.wikipedia.org/wiki/Tennessee_v._Garner
2. https://en.wikipedia.org/wiki/Graham_v._Connor
3. http://www.businessdictionary.com/definition/reasonable-person.html

5. What Type of Spray Should I Buy?

1. https://www.safariland.com/on/demandware.static/-/Sites-tsg-Library/default/dwd4ad6a29/resources/less-lethal/aerosol-reports/oc-and-pepper-sprays.pdf
2. https://www.sabrered.com/formulations-heat-strength-and-law

6. What Are the Laws on Pepper Spray?

1. https://www.atf.gov/resource-center/docs/guide/state-laws-and-published-ordinances-2010-2011-alaska/download
2. https://law.justia.com/codes/arkansas/2010/title-5/subtitle-6/chapter-73/subchapter-1/5-73-124/
3. http://consumerwiki.dca.ca.gov/wiki/index.php/Pepper_Spray_(Mace/Tear_Gas)
4. https://www.flsenate.gov/Laws/Statutes/2017/790.01
5. http://qcode.us/codes/kauaicounty/
6. http://www.legislature.mi.gov/(S(xghhgtxbpgbf2huldjzemhtk))/mileg.aspx?page=GetObject&objectname=mcl-750-224d
7. https://www.atf.gov/resource-center/docs/guide/state-laws-and-published-ordinances-2010-2011-nevada/download
8. http://codes.findlaw.com/ny/penal-law/pen-sect-265-20.html
9. http://lis.njleg.state.nj.us/nxt/gateway.dll?f=templates&fn=default.htm&vid=Publish:10.1048/Enu
10. http://apps.leg.wa.gov/RCW/default.aspx?cite=9.91.160
11. https://docs.legis.wisconsin.gov/statutes/statutes/941/III/26

10. How Do I Decontaminate Others or Myself?

1. Grossman, Dave and Loren W. Christensen. On Combat: The Psychology and Physiology of Deadly Conflict in War and Peace. 2nd ed. PPCT Research Publications, 2007

1. Introduction to Geodesic Domes

1. https://www.bfi.org/about-fuller/big-ideas/geodesic-domes
2. ttps://www.ziptiedomes.com/faq/What-Is-Geodesic-Dome-Frequency-Explained.htm
3. https://issuu.com/golfstromen/docs/lloyd-kahn-1971
4. https://www.lloydkahn.com/

2. Introduction to Ferrrocement

1. https://www.itacanet.org/ferrocement-water-tanks-and-their-construction/
2. http://adkison.name/ferro/ferro_cement_basics.html
3. https://theconstructor.org/concrete/ferrocement-in-construction/1156/
4. https://en.wikipedia.org/wiki/Ferrocement
5. ferrocement.com
6. http://ferrocement.com/intro-Ferro/intro.en.html
7. https://www.mortarsprayer.com/

3. Introduction to Latex Cement

1. https://www.researchgate.net/publication/295675998_Disposing_Waste_Latex_Paints_in_Cement-Based_Materials_-_Effect_on_Flow_and_Rheological_Properties
2. https://www.tngun.com/how-to-build-a-paintcrete-roof-outhouse/

4. Preparing EMT Conduit Spars

1. http://www.desertdomes.com/tips.html
2. http://www.domerama.com/fabricating/making-the-struts/geodesic-dome-struts-flattening/
3. http://www.desertdomes.com/tips.html

5. Assembling the Basic Dome

1. https://www.monolithic.org/products
2. http://www.stuartmcmillen.com/blog/chilling-domes-physics/

7. Adding Ferrocement

1. http://www.mortarsprayer.com/
2. http://www.mortarsprayer.com/spiderlath/
3. http://www.billboardtarps.com/

8. Extra Items

1. http://harmoniouspalette.com/BuildGreen.html

HOW I BUILT A FERROCEMENT "BOULDER BUNKER"

As Seen on Doomsday Preppers

DAVID NASH

1

INTRODUCTION TO GEODESIC DOMES

Geodesic domes stir the imagination of people interested in self-reliance, individuals who want to built more sustainably, or just guys like me that want to DIY and don't have a lot of money.

I needed a secure storage/cabin for some land I bought to use as a "bug-out location" or, as I told my wife, a place to go camping on the weekends.

There are a lot of great reasons for building in the method I have documented.

First off, geodesic domes are amazing marvels of engineering[1], no other man-made structure covers more cubic feet for less material than a dome. They are amazingly strong, and once coated with cement, they are extremely disaster resilient.

Domes are inherently stable, and as you assemble yours, you will find that the triangles that make up the dome are under constant tension, This contributes to their strength.

This high strength and tension between the spars is important if you want to backfill over them. (However, if you want to do cover anything with tons of dirt, I would suggest you use and engineer and not plans from the internet…)

Because you don't need a lot of material to get a good amount of strength, you can build a framework out of cheap material I have had a lot of success out of using EMT conduit from the lumber store. EMT is 4-5 dollars a ten-foot stick, and the dome I built uses 35 such sticks. Because I was building a "Bunker" for a reality show I used ferrocement, but over the years I found an even cheaper solution by the name of Latex Cement. If I had to do this again, I would replace the Ferrocement with Latex Cement, at least for the first few coats. I like ferrocement, and it is a great DIY building technique, but Latex cement is a little easier, especially for a roof.

I will go into greater detail, as well as post some pictures, however, the basics are simple:

8ft tall 16 ft diameter dome:

1. Buy 35 pieces of ¾ inch metal conduit pipe and an engineer's tape measure
2. Cut each pipe into tow pieces one 4.7 feet long the other 5.3 feet long (the engineer tape is marked in tenths of a foot instead of inches)
3. Using a hydraulic press, flatten both ends of the every pipe section. Ensure that the pipe weld is not in the center or edge of the flattened area, and that both flattened ends of each pipe are on the same plane

4. Drill a ¾ inch hole in each flattened end ½ inch from the ends
5. It is helpful to then bend the flattened ends 18 degrees out from the pipe (I just crank down on the pipe when bolting to make the ends bend where they need to go)
6. Bolt the pipes together in triangles using 2.5 inch long ¾ bolts nuts and washers (use the picture diagram in the assembly chapter to see where the long and short pipes go).
7. Cover in several layers of chicken wire
8. Mix Portland cement and sand at a 1/3 ratio of cement and sand with just enough water to get the cement to "slump"
9. Plaster over the chicken wire, either with a sprayer or using one worker inside pressing against the trowel of a worker plastering on the outside
10. Let cure over a couple days
11. Throw motlov cocktails at dome to prove it is strong…. Just kidding the producers of the reality TV show that filmed the making of this dome preferred tannerite. Note: due to the power of the editor, it only looks like my dad was in the "bunker" during the test phase. We don't always get along but I would never put anyone in a building and set off explosives next to it.

Dome Frequency

Domes are best described by their frequency[2]. Historically frequency is denoted by the Greek letter ν. Frequency or ν describes how many divisions are in the dome. It is easiest to think of a dome as a collection of triangles.

If you use a few triangles you will get something like a dome, however it will be closer to a funny looking box.

If you divide the triangle into smaller triangles and push the connections outward, you get a rounder shape. The more divisions you have the closer you get to a true dome.

If you put a dividing line in the center of the 1v triangle, it would break the 1v dome into a 2v dome.

Split it once more, you get a 3v dome.

The more you divide the stronger the dome. However, the more divisions the more complicated the math. It also means more struts of a smaller size. Basically, the more v you add, you have more strut sizes to cut.

If you stay small, a 2v dome is simple. I think it gives a good compromise of 'roundish' shape, and is still relatively simple to build. The 16 foot diameter 2v dome I describe in this book allows me to use 10 foot conduit cut into two pieces with very little waste. I needed:

- 30 4.7ft sections
- 35 5.3 ft sections

Since the EMT comes in 10 feet lengths, I only needed 35 total pieces and had 5 leftover 4.7ft pieces which I used when designing the door.

If we were building the same size dome in 3v it would need 30 2.8ft pieces, 40 40 3.28 pieces, and 50 3.30 pieces

A 6v dome needs 9 different sizes and 555 different sections. A 6v dome is much stronger, and more eye pleasing in its roundness. I wanted simple fast and cheap, so I am satisfied with my 2v dome.

Octahedron and Other Dome Types

There are different types of geodesic dome calculations, some more rounded or flatter on the base than others.

I like Octahedron domes because they are able to be perfectly split down the middle, which works good for making pavilions or starting a tunnel dome.

The icosahedron dome is based off the basic pentagon shape and is the most rounded version of the geodesic dome. Iy has a lot of smaller triangles, so it has great strength. Because of its eye pleasing roundness and high strength it is the most common version of the geodesic dome built commercially. Unfortunately, for the do-it-yourselfer, the amount of spars makes it very complicated to build.

The tetrahedron dome is least circular dome. This is because the triangles are larger and the dome is less complicated. Tt is the weakest dome shape because of this. Therefore it can support the least amount of weight. However, it is the simplest and faster to build.

You also need to understand that a dome is not exactly half a sphere (except maybe with an octahedron). Normally, they are a little more or a little less than half. This is expressed in dome calculators as being either 3/8 or 5/8 domes. In my experience, which your milage may vary, I like to build a 3/8 dome and set it on a short stem wall. A 5/8 is more than half, so it bows out toward the ground and then tightens back up at the very base. I don't like the look personally.

Calculating Dome Materials

Their are some great books on the subject of Geodesic dome math. If you are really into domes you can purchase them and learn to calculate your own sizes.

If you want to join multiple domes together to make things like tunnels you should probably learn the math.

However, there are some great calculators online that will do all the math for you. Some will even calculate things like weight of the base structure, how many square feet of covering you need, and cost.

I have a calculator link page at the end of this document that shows some of the many online calculator options and what I like about the specific sites that contain them.

Problems with Domes

I have a great out of print book called Domebook 2[3] which it, and Domebook 1, have inspired entire generations of dome builders. Lloyd Kahn[4], the author, has build a lot of domes

over the years, has turned against the concepts calling them
"Smart, but not Wise". He noted the following disadvantages:

- Off-the-shelf building materials (e.g., plywood,
  strand board) are rectangular shapes, therefore
  increasing waste and the cost of construction.
- Fire escapes are problematic
- Windows can cost anywhere from five to fifteen
  times as much as windows in conventional houses.
- Wiring costs more because of increased labor time.
- Expansion and partitioning is also difficult. It is hard
  to build a square wall in a round building.
- Kahn notes that domes are difficult to build with
  natural materials, generally requiring plastics, etc.,
  which are polluting and deteriorate in sunlight.

2

INTRODUCTION TO FERRROCEMENT

I have been interested in cheap yet effective building materials for some time. I normally focus my search on what works in developing nations, if a person with third world resources can do make something happen, then a first world inhabitant should be able to do it as well.

I stumbled upon ferrocement from researching water tanks[1]. This is a common and inexpensive method for building them. Also ferrocement has been used to build ships[2].

Basically, all ferrocement[3] is a system of mortar or cement that is applied over a thin metal mesh. Most often this mesh is several layers of chicken wire.

From wikipedia[4], I learned that it was first used in the mid 1840s in France, and it is said it is the basis for reinforced concrete.

I have been using type S mortar in my experiments, and it works well. Type S mortar has a high compressive strength and a good high-tensile bond. I like ti because it works well below grace and handles seismic and wind loads extremely well.

A good source for Ferrocement information is ferrocement.com[5], they have basic mixing proportions[6] Mixing is relatively simple as you are just making a thin shell cement covering a lot of steel. Dry measure it is 3:1 sand to cement mix.

Add water until you can draw a line in it with your finger and it the indent settles slowly. Too much water will reduce your end strength.

If you don't have access to a lot of wire mesh, or you are broke like I am when doing a lot of my experiments, you can substitute other fibers. I have had good success playing with burlap instead of chicken wire. I have also used windows screen. This is called bio-fiber, hempcrete, or burlapcrete depending on what you use.

When making my bunker, I had a lot of help from a really cool device called a Tirolessa sprayer that I got from mortar-sprayer.com[7]. This site has a ton of great information as well as a blog and project advice. I could not have gotten my bunker done on time without the help of guys at this site.

What a Tirolessa is basically a steel bucket with holes at the bottom. An airline is attached to the handle and as air blows through the bottom of the bucket, it picks up the cement slurry and pushes it out of the holes. As you run out of cement, you just dip the bucket into your wheelbarrow of mix. With practice you can spray a lot of cement very quickly. The only drawback is that it takes a pretty powerful air compressor to work well.

It took us a while to find the right mix to get the results I wanted, but a mix of two parts fine sand to one part Portland cement, with enough water to give it a consistency between pea soup and oatmeal works well.

Because a mortar sprayer throws the cement out with some force, it works very well for the first layer of mix. It sticks to the frame work pretty well. After 4 or 5 thin layers the thin shell ferrocement will withstand a blow from a sledgehammer. I can stand on a roof made of this material very easily.

If you overlap your chicken wire so it makes holes about 1/4 in diameter. You can get away with 2 layers, but 4 is better. An interesting fact is that. Chicken wire and cement will expand and contract the same amount with heat and cold which allows thinner sections and less cracking over time.

There isn't a lot of hard and fast rules for ferrocement in the DIY arena. I did a lot of research to see what other people were doing and then took all the ideas and just did it. Its not really all that complicated if you are willing o do the work.

3

INTRODUCTION TO LATEX CEMENT

I first learned about latex roofs while researching ferrocement. While I still like ferrocement as a building material, this particular technique is a little better suited to roofs. The Dept. of Civil and Environmental Engineering, Notre Dame University[1] did an experiment on disposing of latex paint inside of cement to replace the water. This was done to find a way to use waste paint, but it had some interesting benefits.

They found the compressive strength of the cement slightly increased at relatively low latex paint rates. I am not worried about strength, I am wanting the flexibility and slight waterproofing aspects the paint brings.

What I used for Paintcrete Roofs

For my experiments I wanted cheap and easy to find. Like my ferrocement work, I used type s mortar and replaced half of the water with 100% acrylic waste paint. I started with a quart of mis-mixed paint I got on sale, but quickly ran out and had to use some leftover latex bathroom ceiling paint with an anti-mold additive.

Over time, I experimented with different paints until I found that PVA primer paint is pretty cheap and works very well in my applications. Once thing I especially like is that if you need to come back later, Old PVA based paintcrete bonds to new PVA based paintcrete. You may want to paint the old mix first with straight paint if you want a waterproof bond, but it does work.

How I Use Latex Cement

What found works the best, even if it somewhat more expensive, is to staple window screen to the frame of what I am building and then mix the cement into a high slump mix. This means it is runny. It should be able to be poured, but not soupy. Remember, the higher the liquid content is the less strong the finished product will be.

You can poured the first coat on mix on and then spread it lightly with an old broom. I find that pouring it on, lightly brushing it down and pouring new mix over covered mesh and working it down works bests. After each coat, I let it sit for several days until it feels dry. I don't let it completely cure because, for one, that would take months. Secondly, I find that it makes the layers bond better to each other.

Once I get the thickness I want, I reserve the last few layers for a very soupy mix that is mostly paint. This serves to help to coat the mortar mix already on the screen. It self levels and leaves a more waterproof coat.

In the event you want more information I have a series of videos on my site along with a PDF from the US Army Corps of Engineers of Latex Admixtures for Portland Cement[2].

If you want to go directly to the video on Youtube, here is the first three videos on my latex roof outhouse series that shows the roof, by the way, the outhouse is finished and it is quite waterproof and working well:

- https://youtu.be/nLiUigTg_nk
- https://youtu.be/oQiExZhsP4s
- https://youtu.be/dj21qJXmNGI

Additionally, I used this to make a shelter for my rabbit hutches, the more I use this technique the more I like it. Currently, I am building a bamboo based dome and plan on using this technique with burlap to build a large pavilion/outdoor kitchen dome.

4

PREPARING EMT CONDUIT SPARS

I have a youtube video describing the process:

- https://youtu.be/WerkFdf362A

I also have a video showing the jig and how I smashed the ends:

- https://youtu.be/RhBK4J0GgFE

Because of the math, most calculators, and the most accurate builds use tenths of an inch instead of fractions of an inch.

Being new to such a concept, it took me a while to figure out the .3 and .7 of a foot. However, I soon learned that most construction supply stores (like Lowes and Home Depot) carry a specialty engineer's tape measure. This kind of tape has the SAE measurements of ½, ¾ on one side, with the other side showing decimal feet on the other. These tapes do not cost more than traditional tape measures.

In decimal feet, instead of each foot being divided into 12 segments, a decimal foot is divided into 10 segments.

One thing to note, however you decide to measure, when you cut your struts, add whatever length your calculator gives you and add one and a half inches. This allows you to drill your holes 3/4 inch from the pipe ends and still meet your length of strut. With my dome, being the two strut lengths divided to be exactly 10 feet, I could not do this step. It still worked on a 2v dome, the finished product was just slightly smaller than the calculator length and the last few triangles were harder to connect as the entire dome had to shift to make up the difference in size.

In a dome with more frequencies, this would not work, accuracy is very important. Especially as you grow in size and frequency.

Building a Jig

To make the process easier and faster, I made a jig[1], I got the idea from desert domes, I have tried other methods, but this works the best in my opinion.

- I took an 8 foot 2×4, and marked a line down the entire length at 1/3 and 2/3 dividing it into thirds lengthways
- I set my blade at a 45 degree angle, and dropped the blade into the table saw until approximately 1/3 inch remained visible. This allowed a shallow cut.
- I set the table saw bar so that I could slice down the outer lines, and using a saw pusher for safety, I made a cuts that the farthest line on my 2x4 was at the

bottom of the saw blade, and the angled cut was pointed at the center of the board.

- Next I flipped the board and ran it through again, once again ensuring the other far end of the board was at the widest part of the blade. This made a shallow 'v' shaped cut.
- Once I removed the long triangular waste piece, I cut the board at 6 foot and screwed a section of 2×4 to the end to act as a stopper.
- Lastly, I measured and marked two lines at 4.7 inches and 5.3 inches from the stopper. This allowed me to make exact marks on each pipe to ensure they were all cut the same length.

Cutting the Spars

You can use a hacksaw, but I found a LARGE pipe cutter was much easier. The larger the better, and a pipe cutter made it easy to get exacting cuts.

Once all the pipes were cut, I then took a sharpie and marked the weld lines, and a mark about an inch and a half from each end.

Once all of the pipes were cut and marked I was ready to change my jig around and get into the smashing[2] and drilling of the ends of the pipe.

Flattening the Ends of the Spars

I have read that you should not have the weld in the center or on the side of your flattened end. If you drill through the weld it can cause the end it to crack. Since I took the step of marking the weld I simply rotated it 45 degrees from the press and it ended up about 1/3 of the way on the flat end.

There are many ways you can flatten the strut ends: You can hammer them flat, use a large shop vice (reportedly this is destructive to the vice), or use a hydraulic press. I tried them all and decided to use a shop press. I saved up and bought a 12 ton press specifically to make domes. It works well, but I want to add a hydraulic jack instead of a hand pumped jack to save time when making these domes.

I used a sawhorse to set my 2×4 jig parallel to the ground when I had one end of the jug stationed under the end of the press.

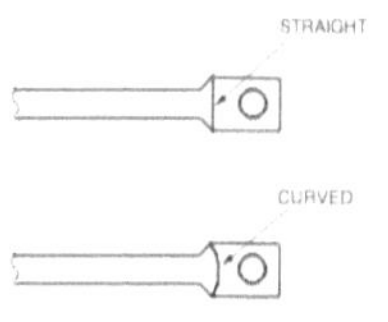

I modified my jig and thinned down one end about 4.1 inches from the stop. This allowed me to place one arbor plate on the 2×4 and line up one end of the plate with the line I marked 1.5 inches from the end That way, each pipe was smashed the exact same amount. Using the arbor plate also allowed me to smash the end with a curve, instead of straight across. This makes each end stronger.

On the desert domes site, they smashed one end of every piece of conduit, drilled it, and then used a bolt screwed into the jig to ensure the other end got flattened on the same plane.

I tried that on the first 10, but found that it was easier and faster if I smashed one end, flipped it over, laid it in the grove, and carefully smashed the other end. I did take the time to ensure that I only smashed the second end after ensuring that everything was lined up and the flat ends were on the same plane. It was not exact, but it was MUCH easier.

Drilling Holes

Once the ends were smashed, I took down the jig, and set it on my drill press, clamped the jig down, and ensured that the hole would be drilled in the center of the flattened conduit end ¾ of an inch from the end.

I used high quality titanium drill bits. This wears out drill bits, my dome used up 2 bits to drill the 130 holes.

Bending the Struts

The triangles don't blot together flat. They bend to make a dome. Most calculators give you the correct angles to bed the ends of your spars. However, I find that in real life the accuracy of the bends is not really important, at least not as important as the length between bolt holes.

In real life, I crank down on the nuts and bolts (using washers so I don't pull through the conduit ends), and the correct angles naturally appear.

Of course, this makes the last few triangles difficult to fit together. To make that process easier, I put everything together very loose, with only a thread or two threaded into the nuts. When I tighten the nuts at the end of the construction cycle I do it in series like putting on a car tire.

However, if you want to come correct, I will add the accurate bending angles for the specific frequencies of domes.

The bending angles[3] are as follows:

- 1v dome: bend 32° on each end
- 2v dome: bend A's 18°, and B's 16° on each end
- 3v dome: bend A's 10°, B's and C's 12° on each end
- 4v dome: bend all struts 7°-9° on each end
- 5v dome: bend all struts 6°-7° on each end
- 6v dome: bend all struts 5°-6° on each end

Painting

Once all the pipes were drilled I painted the ends. I did this to prevent rust where I drilled through the zinc coating, However, the real value was identifying the different lengths of pipe during assembly.

5

ASSEMBLING THE BASIC DOME

I made a Youtube video of the Assembly that you can watch here:

- https://youtu.be/R4Vy8FiOFY8

When I made my first dome I found a great assembly diagram on Mike's Spacetime. This site no longer has the diagram, but here is a representative work.

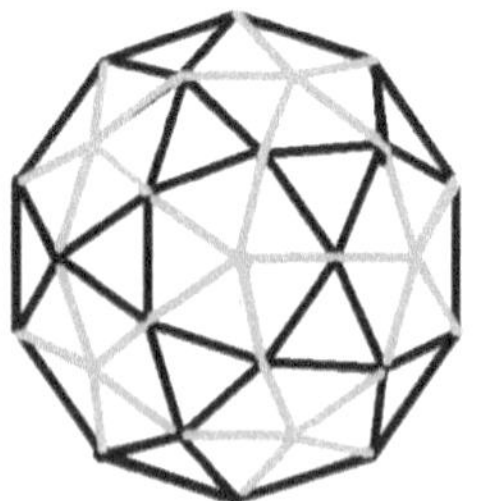

The diagram uses Green and Black for the struts as white doesn't show up on paper, but I used white and black paint

Black designates the long studs in this 2v dome. In this case they are 5.3 feet long.

The Green lines in the diagram represent the short lengths, and they are all 4.3 feet long.

As I said in earlier sections you will need 35 black sections and 20 Green/White sections. I always print this page or draw a large version to nail somewhere near building. The production crew for my Doomsday prepper episode liked the redneckedness of a hand drawn paper nailed to a tree.

I have heard that some people start at the bottom and work up, but in my experience I find starting at the top and working down works best for me.

If you look carefully you will see that a 2v dome is 6 pentagons bolted together, its not assembled that way, but knowing that might make it easier to visualize.

Note: My dad wants me to get a contractor license and allow him to build these domes commercially. I am not interested in the exactness building for pay would require, but if I was to do this, I would build a lot of these pentagons and attach them together and use as a removable form. Similar to how mono-lithic domes[1] use air forms to build domes.

To start, take 5 short struts and bolt them together.

Next take 5 long struts and bolt them to the free ends of your short struts.

Keep everything loose, because as you get closer to having all the short struts bolted to the long struts the center vertices of 5 short struts will have to bow outward.

At each corner of your pentagon, lay out 2 long and one short strut. (Keep the short strut between the two longer struts.)

Now, taking each corner at a time, unbolt a corner and add

the black-green-black struts, and bolt.

Don't tighten the bolts; it is much easier if you keep everything loose until ALL the struts are connected.

If you start at a corner, you will notice that the struts are in the pattern 2 black, 1 green, two black, 1 green. Continue this all the way around. Bolt the side by side black struts together. You will have 5 triangles and 5 short struts radiating out from your pentagon.

LAY OUT 10 short struts around your dome.

Bolt two to the point of each triangle you made in the last step.

Next bolt the free ends of the struts to the short struts from the last step.

As you do this the structure will start to "stand up". I found that it is easier if you have help to lift the top of the structure up, freeing me to pull the struts together.

THIS PART CAN GET a little complicated so feel free to look at the diagram as much as needed.

For the next step you will need 10 long struts and 10 short struts.

Look at the base of structure at each bolt and you will either see 3 short struts (green/white) bolted together OR 2 long struts (black) connected to 2 short (green/white) struts.

At every position with the three short struts lay down 2 more short struts.

At every position where there are 4 struts (2 long, 2 short) lay down 2 long black struts.

Bolt them together in the same way you have done in all the previous steps. Knowing that by this time the dome is wanting to stand up.

I have learned that you can do this by yourself, but extra hands makes this MUCH easier. The first time I built this type of dome, my wife and I put the frame together in about 30 minutes, and she doesn't know the difference in a wrench and a ratchet.

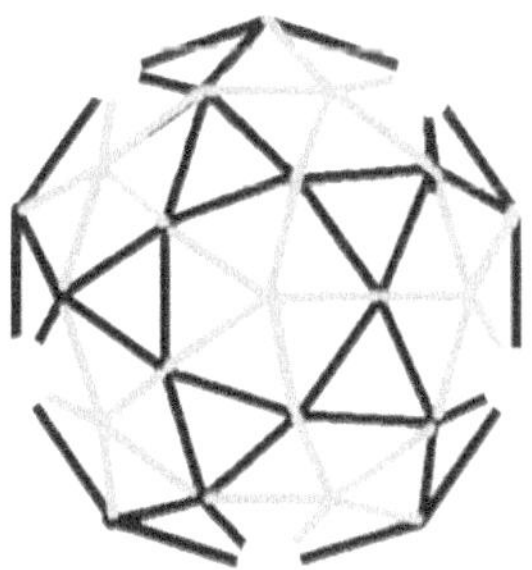

Lastly lay out the last 10 long struts around the base.

These 10 black struts are your base. I find it easiest to start by connecting a short and long strut from the previous step and making a triangle with one of the base struts coming off each side. I then skip the next long and short struts and repeat.

That way I can control the lifting of the dome, and I don't have to lift the entire 150 pounds of conduit pipe each time.

As you come back and connect the struts you skipped, take particular car to ensure that center of each pentagon of short struts is pushed outwards. When we did this the first time, I did not look, and some were pushed inward causing me to have to unbolt entire sections to fix it.

Once everything is assembled you can now tighten the bolts.

You will find that at each vertex (connection) the dome is incredibly strong, however, remember it is only thin walled conduit. The individual pipes are not that strong. I can easily climb the structure if I stay at the connections. I did a pull up in the center of a bar and the bar readily bent.

Remember to stake down the dome, especially if it is a temporary structure using a tarp or parachute covering. The frame is light and will easily blow away.

I did not use any foundation with my dome, which I knew was a mistake, but I was in a hurry to prepare the site for filming.

My later domes are set on some kind of foundation. I like using cinder blocks with a cap block on the bottom and top of the larger block and set over a rubble trench, this allows me to build a wooden floor with a significant gap between the ground and the bottom of the dome. If you do this and allow a small hole at the top of the dome it makes a weird cooling system, which Fuller discovered by accident and explained[2]. This concept is used in nuclear power plants cooling towers.

6

BUILDING A DOOR

Video explaining the door:

- https://youtu.be/rK1F4iVu87k

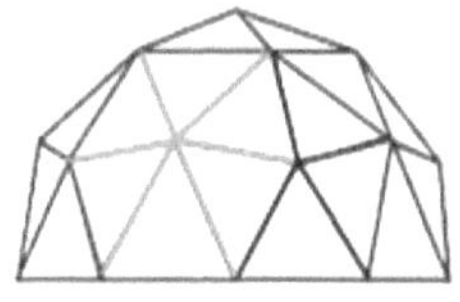

When figuring out the door I got the basic idea from my test build in my front yard, but when my Dad came to help me build the actual cement dome he brought a lifetime of construction experience that I just don't have.

We fiddled around and came up with an idea that I am very happy with but it worked. Unfortunately, due to the time constraints of the film crew we did not write down any measurements, and I could not take video of it.

It has been a main problem with domes to figure out doors. A lot of very popular wood frame construction guides for building a geodome spend a lot of time with how to cut the wooded spars and build the domes, but then totally ignore the door.

However, with the pictures I made on the computer and the experience you will have building the dome, I am sure you can figure it out.

Besides the dome itself, you will need one of the extra 4.3 foot struts, some plumber strap, some nails, and 2x6 boards for the door frame.

We will be working with one of the pentagons.

Pick one that faces the direction you want your door to face (lift the dome and rotate it if needed)

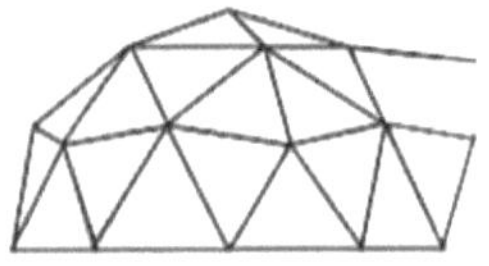

Unbolt the center bolt. Loosed, but do not remove the bolts on the other ends of the struts making the pentagon.

Next, bend the struts outward, as shown in the picture to the left.

Connect the 6 struts into 3 triangles, one at the top, and one on each side of the doorway.

If you want to measure and cut extra conduit you can connect the triangles, but we are just using this to connect to a wood door frame, and are going to wrap welded wire fence over the wood, we elected to leave the triangles "loose".

Frame in the door using traditional carpentry techniques.

We attached the door frame to the conduit pipe using galvanized pipe strapping tape.

We also did not follow this picture exactly, as we did not

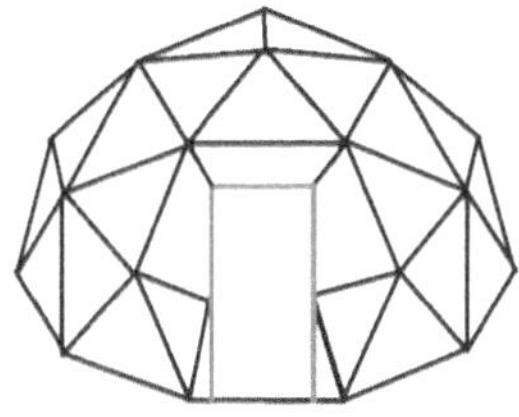

attach the top 2 struts to the corner, but made a triangle that stuck out about 8 inches from the center of the door frame. My goal is to use this to attach a security camera or light to this, as well as to make a small over-hang to reduce rain on whoever is unlocking the door.

This picture shows the rough process, we had not leveled the frame yet, nor finished wrapping all the wire to the frame.

You can, however, see the top triangle sticking out over the door frame.

Something I did not take pictures of, but I think is very important was we took steps to strengthen the door.

In my opinion, there is no sense in making a hardened building with a weak door. A door is only as strong as its frame. If the only thing holding my frame in the cement dome was a couple inches of pipe hanger strap, then a few blows with a sledge will take it out.

Once the door frame was mounted in the 2x6 frame, we drilled several 3/8 holes through the outer and inner frame. Next we threaded long (over a foot long) carriage bolts and bolted the two frames together using a large washer and a locking nut. We then threaded on other nuts and sandwiched in more large washers on the bolts to give purchase to the cement. We also invested a lot of rebar tie wire to connect the long bolts to the fencing and poultry netting. Our hope is that the cement will bond to the bolts as it does with rebar so that the door is integrated with the cement dome.

7

ADDING FERROCEMENT

I shot a video of this to explain the process:

- https://youtu.be/i-ujBh-s-Vg

This was the hardest part of the entire project so far. This was my first attempt at working with cement (other than using a couple bags of ready mix to set fence poles). To make matters worse, We were being filmed by a crew from Doomsday Preppers so we were on an extreme time limit (basically we had one day to do all the cement work), I only had one helper (Thanks Dad), and my mixer kept breaking (note to all owners of a harbor freight mixer, use locktite)…

All in all, I am pleased with the outcome, and learned a lot about what to do, what not to do, and how I would do it if I ever do it again….

What we did up to this point was to build out dome and frame in the door. Now we have to prepare for the cement.

Our intent is to cover the dome using a concept called ferrocement (FC). In ferro-cement you don't have to use as much cement to cover a structure because you are using more structural wire, the ideal is chicken wire every ¼ inch or stucco mesh.

In most instances of using FC workers use a thick mix of Portland cement and sand 1/3 ratio, and work against each other to press a low slump (little water) mix against the wire.

This is very labor intensive, and since I just did not have time, I contacted Nolan Scheid from MortarSprayer.com[1]. His air powered sprayer really saved the project.

I will say, that in my ignorance I did most everything wrong at LEAST once, but his Sprayer enabled me to complete the job on time (well, that and my Dad's labor)

I don't want this article to sound like an advertisement for his sprayer, but I cannot express how vital it was to this process.

That being said, since my budget was too small to afford stucco mesh or enough chicken wire to wrap it 4 times to get the ¼ inch between wires, and I did not know about spider lath[2] at the time of my project, I was worried about the sprayed cement blowing through the wire. (I learned later that it depends a lot on your technique).

So I listened to my father and allowed my fears to modify the plan somewhat by adding some surplus billboard tarps[3] I bought online these tarps are old vinyl billboards and are extremely thick and durable. I originally got these for a pond project, but I was too lazy to hand dig it. I think I got them for under $30.

My original plan was to wrap the dome in welded wire fencing, then the tarp, then the chicken wire, but on site, we began over thinking and changed to covering the frame with the tarp, then fencing, then the 1 inch poultry netting. The thought was that this would allow the cement to get the benefit of the extra iron in the fencing. This caused problems when we started spraying (more about that later).

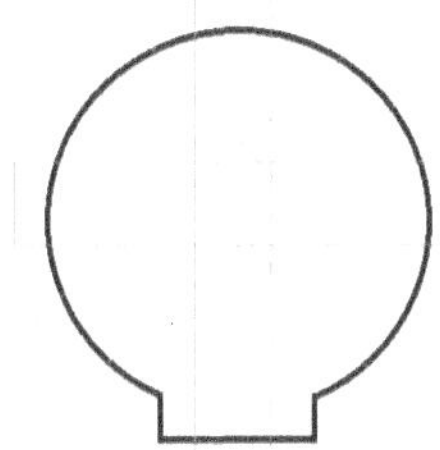

The way we used the fence wire was to divide the ground perimeter of the dome (54 feet) in half and cut the welded fencing wire into 27 foot (plus a little extra) sections. We allowed the wire to roll back up into a loose roll. Next we bent one end back about 6 inches, pressed it under the base of the dome, and the used long poles to push the roll up and over the highest point of the dome.

We did this several times, each time pushing several inches of each end under the base of the dome to give us attachment points when we pour the slab.

We also pulled the fence wire as tight as we could to keep it tight against the dome frame.

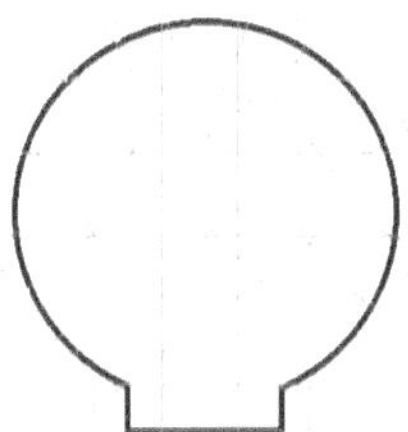

We cut left over fencing wire into 5 or 6 foot lengths and attached that wherever the long rolls did not overlap. We used rebar wire tires to tightly attach it.

We also took a section about 15 foot long and rolled it over the door frame section to make and "igloo" type door.

It was hard to keep everything tight and round, my Dad did a wonderful job of pressing down on the raised sections using a 2x2ft section of plywood and tied everything down smooth while perched on a walk-board. (I blame my dislike of heights on watching too much MacGyver in middle school)…

Next we wrapped one 55 foot length of fence wire around the base, and the forced it to fit the frame. The wire will want to stand straight up, but the dome slopes inward.

It took a lot of fighting and much wire to get the wire nice and flat.(we used a whole 1000 tie bundle of rebar wire ties on this small dome.)

You cannot tell the work put into making the dome smooth with the finished project because of the burlap roles that are supposed to "camouflage" the building, but when we do the inside, the work will show in a much smoother surface.

Next we wrapped the entire dome in Chicken wire, doubling it up so as to get as close as we could to a wire every ¼ inch.

It took us two full days to get to this part. It should not have taken this long, but we had to work with the film crew. They wanted to reshoot several key parts over and over to give the editors things to work with. (I am not complaining, just giving an overview of why a 1 day job took 2.) We did get to mix ONE load of cement that first day. I must admit, that that was the first time I had ever mixed cement, and was unfamiliar with how to use a cement mixer, the result would have been comical, if I was not worried about not getting the dome done in the time allotted. (note: I was not worried about finishing the dome, I knew that would happen. I just did not want the film crew to leave and have it edited to look like a failure).

Luckily for my stress level, the next day the film crew had to film someone else, leaving my Dad and I one whole day to work the cement.

Unfortunately we had to hash out the stress of the previous day before starting to work, and my mixer broke after just a couple of batches. (While the instructions on the Harbor freight mixer do not mention it, put Loctite and a lock washer on the driveshaft that runs the actual mixer barrel, both sides).

Being out in the COUNTRY going to the nearest hardware store took an hour and a half, during which time, my Dad hand mixed the cement to the specifications mentioned on Nolan's Mortar Sprayer website. His cement mix worked MUCH better than mine.

We were able to spray the concrete using the sprayer, and it saved our bacon, but as I mentioned earlier my change in the structure caused problems when we began to spray. What happened was that any cement that blew through the wire (I started with too the PSI set too high, and did not have the sprayer close enough to the wire). The cement then collected on the tarp causing it to bulge out away from the wire. I should have gone with the original plan of laying the tarp over the stronger welded wire fencing and just using the chicken wire for reinforcement. It would have worked better, and the conduit dome frame could have been removed later.

If found that by getting closer to the wire, more stuck to it, but since I was running out of time, and because the camera crew wanted the dome to be camouflaged to look like a boulder (Hey look, a boulder. I wonder how it got the skylights, solar panels, and big metal door...) I wrapped burlap into the chicken wire which helped catch the sprayed mortar. it also allowed me to sculpt the dome so that it had "wrinkles" and boulder like features. This did have an effect on the strength of the dome, but after the dome cures, I will tear out the tarp and spray and plaster the inside of the dome with more cement so that I get more cement into the wire. Hopefully this will make up for the strength I lost.

Luckily we were able to get everything done in time, because while I thought I would have Friday morning to do any last minute tough ups, the film crew hired a painter to paint the dome like a boulder.

He did a great job, and used all sorts of nice grey shades, so instead of a nice cement grey "boulder" we have a nice painted grey "boulder"

I don't want to sound snarky though, because I really am happy with the project, and once I get a round "tuit" and finish the dome, I think it will make a great small classroom for when my range gets built, as it is very close to where we will set up our pistol range.

Until that happens, it gives me a lockable space to keep tools and camping materials for when we spend time on the property getting it ready.

8

EXTRA ITEMS

Water Bottle Skylight

Before we added the chicken wire (which I found that professionals call poultry or avian netting), we installed the two skylights.

(The picture shows a bottle that is not full enough. In actuality the bottle works best completely full, but probably not in the winter if you have hard freezes).

The bottles don't look all that nice, and I got a lot of questioning glances from both the film crew and my Dad (he is a perfectionist when it comes to building), but when the cement dried, and we took off the plastic bags we put on it while spraying cement, they were all amazed at how well it worked.

I have a video showing the process on Youtube: https://youtu.be/M1vZSE7aPJ0

Conduit for Later Wiring

We also took the time to install plastic conduit so that we can come back later to run electricity to the building. When we made the door, we build an 'igloo' style door to create a roofline.

I plan on eventually adding a solar panel to that roofline, but My dad wants to put it on a moveable stand so it can track the sun. He is probably right, but I think my way will look cooler – In the end, we will probably make a stand.

Rain Catchment System

The last adventure in building gizmos was to create a "rain catchment system".

The Doomsday Prepper guys were the big push for this. I was not really sold on the idea, but I like to please, especially when someone else is buying the materials.

In doing my ferrocement research I found a cool website where a guy added planters[1] to his dome (this is an awesome idea and is worth a look). I figure that if my rain catchment system fails (and since it is not level it WILL fail). I will use it to plant blackberries or Muscadine grapes to cover up the dome, even though I will have to be careful about the plants creating cracks in the dome.

Having vines growing up over the dome will help camouflage it, because you can see the dome off of the Natchez Trace Parkway, a big grey "bunker" is not really that covert.

Doomsday Preppers

If you want to see the actual "dome of doom" video that Nat Geo shot of my dome build, it is on youtube:

* https://youtu.be/HF_XmwpvBxk

Additionally, I tried my first google hangout after the show aired and I talked about how the reality show process impacted my build. It is also on youtube:

* https://youtu.be/ePMicE-oVy4

If you are really into this doom of dome, I have a link to blog talk radio where I did a podcast on the process:

* https://urlzs.com/xQQyJ

9

LINKS TO CALCULATORS AND RESOURCES

Zip Tie Domes: I think this is one of the best calculators around. Also, this Tennessee based company has patented a really ingenious system of making domes. Their PVC pipe domes are very inexpensive and are easy to build.

- https://urlzs.com/6cLEs

Desert Domes is the calculator I used when making the dome in this document. I found them first when researching domes and they have a good set of tips, especially for bamboo domes.

- https://urlzs.com/TQN6B

Domerama is another mainstay in the DIY Geodome world. I have spent a lot of time on their hub connector page in search of other ways to build domes.

- https://urlzs.com/m1FaA

Geo-Dome also has a good selection of calculators, I especially like their snow and wind load calculators.

- https://urlzs.com/hzjNR

NOTES

1. Introduction

1. https://shepherdpublish.com/self-published-works/21-days-to-basic-preparedness/

2. Personal Preparedness Mindset

1. https://www.tngun.com/completed-incremental-disaster-kit/

3. Types of Emergency Kits

1. https://www.tngun.com/prn-40-alphabet-kits/

6. Must Have Essentials for a Get Home Bag

1. https://en.wikipedia.org/wiki/Mors_Kochanski
2. https://www.tngun.com/list-of-edc-lists/
3. https://www.tngun.com/essential-gear-for-a-get-home-bag/

Introduction

1. **https://www.tngun.com**

1. What is Pepper Spray?

1. **http://www.historyofwar.org/articles/weapons_metsubishi.html**
2. **https://www.smithsonianmag.com/history/forgotten-history-mace-designed-29-year-old-and-reinvented-police-weapon-180953239/**

3. What is the Proper Mindset?

1. https://en.wikipedia.org/wiki/Tennessee_v._Garner
2. https://en.wikipedia.org/wiki/Graham_v._Connor
3. http://www.businessdictionary.com/definition/reasonable-person.html

5. What Type of Spray Should I Buy?

1. https://www.safariland.com/on/demandware.static/-/Sites-tsg-Library/default/dwd4ad6a29/resources/less-lethal/aerosol-reports/oc-and-pepper-sprays.pdf
2. https://www.sabrered.com/formulations-heat-strength-and-law

6. What Are the Laws on Pepper Spray?

1. https://www.atf.gov/resource-center/docs/guide/state-laws-and-published-ordinances-2010-2011-alaska/download
2. https://law.justia.com/codes/arkansas/2010/title-5/subtitle-6/chapter-73/subchapter-1/5-73-124/
3. http://consumerwiki.dca.ca.gov/wiki/index.php/Pepper_Spray_(Mace/Tear_Gas)
4. https://www.flsenate.gov/Laws/Statutes/2017/790.01
5. http://qcode.us/codes/kauaicounty/
6. http://www.legislature.mi.gov/(S(xghhgtxbpgbf2huldjzemhtk))/mileg.aspx?page=GetObject&objectname=mcl-750-224d
7. https://www.atf.gov/resource-center/docs/guide/state-laws-and-published-ordinances-2010-2011-nevada/download
8. http://codes.findlaw.com/ny/penal-law/pen-sect-265-20.html
9. http://lis.njleg.state.nj.us/nxt/gateway.dll?f=templates&fn=default.htm&vid=Publish:10.1048/Enu
10. http://apps.leg.wa.gov/RCW/default.aspx?cite=9.91.160
11. https://docs.legis.wisconsin.gov/statutes/statutes/941/III/26

10. How Do I Decontaminate Others or Myself?

1. Grossman, Dave and Loren W. Christensen. On Combat: The Psychology and Physiology of Deadly Conflict in War and Peace. 2nd ed. PPCT Research Publications, 2007

1. Introduction to Geodesic Domes

1. https://www.bfi.org/about-fuller/big-ideas/geodesic-domes
2. ttps://www.ziptiedomes.com/faq/What-Is-Geodesic-Dome-Frequency-Explained.htm
3. https://issuu.com/golfstromen/docs/lloyd-kahn-1971
4. https://www.lloydkahn.com/

2. Introduction to Ferrrocement

1. https://www.itacanet.org/ferrocement-water-tanks-and-their-construction/
2. http://adkison.name/ferro/ferro_cement_basics.html
3. https://theconstructor.org/concrete/ferrocement-in-construction/1156/
4. https://en.wikipedia.org/wiki/Ferrocement
5. ferrocement.com
6. http://ferrocement.com/intro-Ferro/intro.en.html
7. https://www.mortarsprayer.com/

3. Introduction to Latex Cement

1. https://www.researchgate.net/publication/295675998_Disposing_Waste_Latex_Paints_in_Cement-Based_Materials_-_Effect_on_Flow_and_Rheological_Properties
2. https://www.tngun.com/how-to-build-a-paintcrete-roof-outhouse/

4. Preparing EMT Conduit Spars

1. http://www.desertdomes.com/tips.html
2. http://www.domerama.com/fabricating/making-the-struts/geodesic-dome-struts-flattening/
3. http://www.desertdomes.com/tips.html

5. Assembling the Basic Dome

1. https://www.monolithic.org/products
2. http://www.stuartmcmillen.com/blog/chilling-domes-physics/

7. Adding Ferrocement

1. http://www.mortarsprayer.com/
2. http://www.mortarsprayer.com/spiderlath/
3. http://www.billboardtarps.com/

8. Extra Items

1. http://harmoniouspalette.com/BuildGreen.html

ADDITIONAL RESOURCES

I wanted to keep this document short and as an easy first steps guide, but if you are interested in learning more,

I have included links to free articles from my site that are related to the concepts you have read about here:

- **Why Have a Personal Preparedness Mindset**
- **Why We Prepare**
- **Dealing with Family that Doesn't Understand Emergency Preparedness**
- **$10 Weekly Food Storage Program**
- **Introduction to Emergency Kits**
- **Bulk Food Storage Using Mylar Bags**
- **Water Storage**
- **DIY Bucket Water Filter**
- **Pool Shock for Water Purification**
- **Firearm Safety**
- **Firearms for Catastrophic Disasters**
- **Should You Shoot to Wound or to Kill?**
- **Communications Plan**

AFTERWORD

If prepping makes your life difficult, then you are not doing it right.

Prepping is life insurance, it is common sense, and it should make you sleep easier at night.

I sincerely hope you have learned something from this small booklet, and that it has given you information that will cause you to take longer steps down the road to a more self-reliant lifestyle.

Please Leave a Review on Amazon it helps others find this book as well as helps me become a better writer.

PLEASE REVIEW

Please visit my Amazon Author Page at:

https://amazon.com/author/davidnash

if you like my work, you can really help me by publishing a review on Amazon.

The link to review this work at Amazon is:

https://www.amazon.com/review/create-review?asin=B07WPPSMQG

BONUS: EXCERPT FROM THE NEW INSTRUCTOR SURVIVAL GUIDE

I never had a problem speaking in public, it scares me, but I have things to say so I just plow on through the fear. It has been my ability to ignore that mean little voice that says things like "They are all going to laugh at you","You can't do it," or "Don't be different" that has led to my success.

Led to, in this case means is the first factor; there is a trainload of things I do to prepare to teach in order to ensure that:

- They don't laugh
- I *can* do it
- Being different leads to innovation

I look at life as a series of trails, as you end one you select another. In the end of your travels each trail contributes to your final destination. For me, being an Instructor was the path that most significantly impacted my final destination. Seeing a student gain knowledge that leans to change is what drives me. Sharing information is what I am addicted to. Nothing is better than when someone tells me what I taught them helped.

Being an instructor in a classroom was my start. Teaching courses led to becoming a video content creator, a podcaster, and an author. I don't distinguish between the ways to share knowledge, I only judge on the effectiveness of the method for the student at hand.

I am a primarily a firearm instructor. I teach other things, but firearm instruction is my primary skillset. It doesn't matter what your skill is, as the science of adult education is the same. Most people begin their instructor process by getting certified as an instructor in whatever skill they are most interested in. For firearms, that means the NRA. I taught some "hip-pocket" classes in the Marines, and I liked teaching younger guys the ropes, but I never thought about instructing until I saw an advertisement for a NRA Instructor course. I sold some things to make the tuition and took my first NRA instructor course. It was 17 hours long, and did a good job at teaching me how to teach the NRA lesson plan.

What is did not teach me was everything else I needed to know to run a training business. It took me a year after the course to feel comfortable teaching the course curriculum. It took me much longer than that to get a system in place to run a business

Being an instructor gets in your blood, but it is not something you can learn in a weekend course, no matter how good it is.

In this document I want to share things that helped me as I got started so that you don't have all the growing pains I suffered.

If you are interested in the The New Instructor Survival Guide, you can find it on Amazon.

ALSO BY DAVID NASH

Fiction

The Deserter: Legion Chronicles Book 1

The Revolution: Legion Chronicles Book 2

Non Fiction

21 Days to Basic Preparedness

52 Prepper Projects

52 Prepper Projects for Parents and Kids

52 Unique Techniques for Stocking Food for Preppers

Basic Survival: A Beginner's Guide

Building a Get Home Bag

Handguns for Self Defense

How I Built a Ferrocement "Boulder Bunker"

New Instructor Survival Guide

The Basics of Raising Backyard Chickens

The Prepper's Guide to Foraging

The Prepper's Guide to Foraging: Revised 2nd Edition

The Ultimate Guide to Pepper Spray

Understanding the Use of Handguns for Self Defense

Note and Record Books

Correction Officer's Notebook

Get Healthy Notebook

Rabbitry Records

Collections and Box Sets

Preparedness Collection

Translations

La Guía Definitiva Para El Spray De Pimienta

Multimedia

Alternative Energy

Firearm Manuals

Military Manuals 2 Disk Set

ABOUT THE AUTHOR

 David Nash is a former Marine with over a decade of experience in Emergency Management and another ten years in Corrections. He currently works in training as an instructor at a correction academy teaching new officers how to handle angry felons.

Add in a couple of semesters working in a liquor store during college and he has seen it all. In fact, David had the third highest prepper score on the NatGeo show Doomsday Preppers as well as worked more than 20 Presidentially declared disasters.

He has authored several books on preparedness, as well as worked on several disaster response plans as a state planner.

He is a father and a husband. He enjoys time with his young son William Tell and his school teacher wife Genny. When not working, writing, creating content for YouTube, playing on his self-reliance blog, or smoking award-winning BBQ he is asleep.

amazon.com/author/davidnash

facebook.com/booksbynash

youtube.com//tngun

goodreads.com/david_allen_nash

twitter.com/dnash1974

instagram.com/shepherdschool

pinterest.com/tngun